W9-AVR-405

How to Live in Hawaii on $1,000 Per Month

How to Live in Hawaii on $1,000 Per Month

By

Yolanda J. Benhan

Copyright © 1994, 2000 by Yolanda J. Benham

All rights reserved.
No part of this book may be reproduced, stored in a retrieval system, or transmitted by any means, electronic, mechanical, photocopying, recording, or otherwise, without written permission from the author.

ISBN: 1-58721-580-2

Printed in the United States of America

First printing   1995
Second revision 1999
Third revision   2000

*First published in 1999 by Rico Press,
Kailua-Kona, Hawaii*

1stBooks - rev. 9/12/00

About The Book

New Book updated for 2000-"How to Live in Hawaii for $1000 Per Month." Complete guide to living and vacationing in an affordable paradise. In depth housing information for buying and renting, detailed costs of living, recreation, health care, tips on moving, even business opportunities. Featuring a list of Hawaii's 1,000 major employers, addresses, and phone numbers. The most comprehensive and resourceful description available. Covers the islands of Oahu, Maui, Kauai, and the Big Island of Hawaii. This book has earned dozens of letters of praise and "thank you's" from its readers.

TABLE OF CONTENTS

FOREWORD

My great, great grandparents settled in the Hawaiian islands in 1839 when it was still a kingdom. I was born in Hawaii before it became a state, and did not leave the islands for Southern California until I was sixteen. Having grown up in what is probably the most beautiful spot on earth, with the world's best climate, I took it all for granted and assumed the rest of the world was not much different. Surprise! I soon learned otherwise.

Later I married and traveled around the world through Europe, South America, and the Orient. Athough we tried living in other places (California, Nevada, Florida), we always became homesick. Like so many other transplanted Hawaiians, we still heard the song of the islands. It proved to be too strong to resist, calling the wanderers to return home. We greet the sun's rays every morning with a glad heart. It's so good to be back.

In 1992, I was visiting my cousin in Lahaina on the island of Maui where I spoke with a tourist in a supermarket. When he found out that I live here, gesturing at the high-priced groceries he asked incredulously: "You mean you actually **live** here? " Then he blurted out, "How can you afford it?" I thought about his question for a moment. Since he was in a hurry to catch an airplane and it would have taken a long time to answer his query, I just smiled in response and waved goodbye.

Realizing that there must be many more traffic-snarled, smog-choked, crime-weary urbanites out there who would like to know how they, too, could afford to live here, his question prompted this book. Almost anyone who has experienced Hawaii would like to know the answer to his question. I hope that when you finish reading it, you, too, will want to see this isle of golden dreams. And if living here becomes your dream, then this book will help you make it come true.

INTRODUCTION

Yes, we know that you've heard that living in Hawaii is expensive - the cost of housing, either to buy or to rent, is sky high. Food, gasoline, and other items are imported and therefore costly. That's all true enough. Hawaii **is** expensive for the tourists who frequent Waikiki, Lahaina, and the other tourist traps, or those who choose to live on Oahu with its traffic jams and nearly a million people vying for space.

The Other Hawaii

Yet there is another Hawaii, virtually undiscovered, or at least not well publicized, which is about as close to Paradise as you can get on the face of this earth, where residents live comfortably on modest incomes. These areas are known only to local inhabitants and the few fortunate souls who have discovered a retirement Eden (and would like to keep it quiet). Several folks I spoke with about this book were irate at the thought that it might attract more residents.

Why consider living in a Third World country when you can live in or retire to a Hawaiian Eden? Have you ever tried to cash a check in a Costa Rican bank? You can stand in line for hours. Some people even make a living standing in line for others! Here you have the protection of U.S. laws and no money changing problems. Here you can understand the language, you can enjoy good medical care, F.D.A. inspected food, and you can drink the water! Here you can enjoy American supermarkets and products, friendly neighbors, and all in a virtually **crime free** environment!

Up-to-date information will be disclosed, and little known Hawaiian towns will be evaluated from the viewpoint of factors important to basic living: (1) climate (2) cost of living (3) availability and cost of housing (4) medical facilities (5) business and job opportunities (6) recreation and cultural activities. The fabled island of Hawaii is less than a five hour flight from California, and travel time is getting shorter. If you choose to do so, this book will help you to live joyously where Americans have dreamed of retiring for years.

Incidentally, we've heard visitors say, apologetically, that they can't seem to pronounce Hawaiian words. Don't be put off by the Hawaiian words in this text. They're not as hard to say as they seem at first glance, and we've included a pronunciation guide for you that will soon have you speaking like a native. Well, almost. (See Appendix A).

For anyone who thinks he or she might like to live in Hawaii, I recommend that you subscribe beforehand to one of the two daily island newspapers - the **Hawaii Tribune Herald** for East Hawaii, and **West Hawaii Today.** Their addresses and phone numbers are given on Page 47. If you read these local papers, particularly the classifieds, you'll keep current with rentals and sales prices of housing, household furnishings, and appliances.

The world news coverage is exceptional for such small town newspapers. Local news will reveal community concerns. Letters to the Editor air complaints and the opinions of the opinionated that can give you insight into local politics, where to go and what to do when you get here.

This book is intended to be a "how to" book, that is how to afford to live here if you decide to stay, and what to do and where to go on a visit or extended stay. Recognizing that firms go in and out of business and personnel change, recommendations given are an endorsement only of the specific individuals named.

Please note that prices quoted in this book, and phone numbers given, although current are subject to change over time. The opinions expressed are those of the author.

Map of the
Hawaiian Islands

hiihau Kauai

Oahu

Molokai

Maui

Lanai

Kahoolawe

Kailua
Kona   Hilo . Hilo
                              Bay

Hawaii
The Big Island

CHAPTER 1 - THE HAWAIIAN ISLANDS

Eons ago, undersea volcanic activity began to push up the many islands comprising the Hawaiian chain. Located roughly 2,400 miles Southwest of Los Angeles (as the mynah bird flies), visitors know primarily the six main large islands:

1. Northernmost Kauai, the so-called Garden Island, with its abundant rainfall and greenery, the site of rough hurricanes that pound its northern coast approximately every ten years.
2. Oahu, upon which the sophisticated capital city of Honolulu is a hustling beehive of activity, home to nearly a million inhabitants.
3. Slumbering Molokai, with its towering cliffs sheltering a land that time forgot.
4. Little Lanai, with its red dirt and golden sugar cane fields, site of two of the most expensive resort hotels in the world.
5. Maui, whose radiant beauty has brought her worldwide renown.
6. Hawaii, also known as the Big Island, the Southernmost island whose brooding presence is home to Pele, the Hawaiian Goddess of the Volcano.

Hawaii had its own rulers and governed itself very well until 1898, when the United States, with gun-boat diplomacy, forced Queen Liliuokalani to hand over her kingdom. If it hadn't been the United States, one of the other great colonial powers, Germany, France, England or Russia, would have taken it over. Since the takeover was inevitable (guns win out over spears every time), out of the five possible ruling countries, Hawaii hit the jackpot. In fact, we were having dinner a few years back with Costa Rican friends in San Jose. When I briefly recounted this history of Hawaii, our dinner companion, a Costa Rican doctor, said wistfully: "I wish Costa Rica had been taken over by the United States." I was stunned and remember that remark when I read about Hawaiian activists wanting to return to Hawaiian self-rule.

Evidently many visitors agreed with Mark Twain's description of Hawaii as "the most beautiful fleet of islands anchored in any ocean," and decided to stay. Since the land is scarce and the demand for land is great, Oahu now is high priced and overcrowded. Each island (except Oahu) offers opportunities for low cost living, but perhaps the most affordable today is the Big Island.

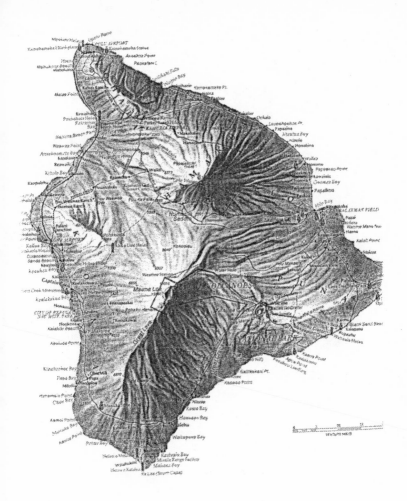

Hawaii

3

CHAPTER 2. HAWAII, THE BIG ISLAND

Lying approximately 200 miles Southeast of Oahu, the Big Island is farthest away from Honolulu, and the last to be commercialized. East Hawaii and its town of Hilo is fairly well developed with hotels, shopping centers, and a small industrial base, having started its growth in the 1800's. Hilo also controls the political base of the island, with West Hawaii somewhat of a step-sister.

A lack of water sources slowed construction in West Hawaii. Widespread business activities began there only in this century, and the Kohala-Kona Coast is in about the same stage of development that Oahu was in fifty years ago. Much water has been discovered recently, enough potentially to sustain growth for another 50 - 100 years. Large housing projects are in the planning stage. Retailers have discovered its potential, and huge discount houses have recently been built, including the largest K-Mart and Wal-Mart stores in the islands which are now open for business. Home Depot is considering opening a branch in Kona.

The Keahole-Kona runway extension has just been completed, making it possible for jumbo jets to fly directly to Kona from Chicago and other Eastern cities in the U.S. We can expect increased traffic from the Orient and other Pacific Rim gateway cities as well. These jets will carry an increased passenger load - up to 550, nearly twice as much as the venerable DC-10.

Additional visitors will soon discover the incomparable climate of the Big Island, the wonder of this breathtaking world of green pastures and roving herds, of dazzling azure seas, of brilliant blue skies padded by puffy white cotton clouds. When they feel the intoxication of soft breezes redolent with the perfume of ginger and gardenias, and also learn that the area is virtually **crime free**, then many more visitors will fall in love with the island of Hawaii, and decide to call it home.

Crime Free?

As you well know, violent crime is rampant on the mainland, especially in large cities, and many live in constant fear of becoming victims. Oahu's crime rate has greatly increased with its burgeoning population. The island of Hawaii, on the other hand, is known for its peace and quiet, and its almost total absence of violent crime. Here residents sleep without fear. Why is this so?

The island population is geographically limited. Visitors can't drive here, as they do to other states. They have to fly or take a boat. That costs money. So crowds are geographically, or economically, if you will, excluded.

Because there are only 120,000 or so residents on the entire island, there are few violent crimes. These consist mostly of DUI's and domestic arguments. Also, there are only two major airports on the island. If a crime is committed, the coconut wireless is remarkably efficient, and guess who will be waiting at the airports? Hawaii's finest, that's who.

Incidentally, the job of police officer on the island is a great one, but watch your speed limit. They have to have something to do besides taking coffee breaks and shuffling paperwork. This is said partly in jest, of course. Actually, the local police officers are amazingly polite and helpful.

Policemen on the island number approximately 430, one for every 279 residents. Typically, murder and non-negligent manslaughter offenses number less than 10 per year. What does keep the department hopping is the increase in traffic accidents, which tripled between 1988 and 1991, and since then has more than kept pace with increased population growth.

Since the island is so sparsely populated, people seem to recognize each other by first name, and the old-time virtues of being reluctant to bring dishonor on one's self and one's family, of being **known** in the community, serve to deter wrongdoing. We are rarely bothered by petty thievery, there's no graffiti, unless you count the messages and names written in white coral on black lava fields, and no gang warfare.

On the Big Island, we've enjoyed a wonderful, laid-back, open and friendly lifestyle, seldom bothering to lock doors and windows and our cars. This carefree lifestyle has been brought to an abrupt end by a rash of burglaries on the island during the summer of 1999. Police are blaming the increased numbers of drug addicts and are now huffing and puffing to keep up with 911 calls. They're advising everyone to lock houses and cars. We still enjoy peaceful surroundings, walk and ride around the island unafraid of violence, but now it's prudent to lock windows and doors.

Basically, more population brings with it the three evils of city life - crime, pollution, and traffic jams. Fifty and even forty years ago Oahu was also a wonderful place to live, where residents rarely locked their doors, and the virtues of small town America existed. The crush of close to a million people ended that lifestyle.

Right now, right here, today, and perhaps for another twenty years or so, you can enjoy peace and tranquility on the Big Island as it existed in Honolulu, Oahu and in many other smaller towns in the United States forty years ago. And this is true of the entire Big Island. Appealing? You bet it is. This factor alone is making many people pack their bags Hawaii bound.

The Weather

Picture yourself living in the best possible climate in the world, winter or summer. In most areas of the United States, it is either so cold in the winter, or so hot in the summer, that residents feel they need to get away during the bad weather months and take a break. The only bad weather Hawaii has is rainfall, and even that is warm. Herein lies Hawaii's charm. Its climate is simply superb.

There's a virtual exodus to Hawaii and Florida during the winter months, when snowbird tourists attempt to escape shoveling snow and sliding over icy streets. Then in summer, there's a reverse exodus from the southern and midwestern states, when summer heat drives residents to the mountains or seashore. Vegans and Angelenos try to escape not only the heat, but the smog as well. Hawaiians never feel the need to escape from heat or cold, and the air they breathe is fresh and pure. In local parlance, "Lucky you live Hawaii!"

The Pacific Ocean acts as a moderating influence, and the weather along the shoreline doesn't change much during the year. It remains a boring 70 to 80 degrees. Isn't that hard to take? With alternating mountain and ocean trade winds, shorts and a tee shirt are comfortable year round. And if it seems a bit warm, cooling shade is always nearby under a coconut or banyan tree, or you can jump in the ocean for a quick swim to cool off. (If you prefer cooler weather, head for the hills).

Despite this sameness of climate, there's an astonishing variety of different microclimates on the island - from tropical rainforest to high and low desert. Since the temperature drops about three degrees for every thousand feet of higher altitude, you can pick and choose your preferred climate and ocean view, by altitude.

Since weather here is largely determined by altitude, at ocean level, the climate is summer year-round. A moderate elevation, say 1,000 feet, is year-round spring. The higher you go, the cooler it gets. You'll need a sweater or light jacket at higher elevations. You'll want to dress in layers, so you can peel off at the beach or slip into a sweater to visit the volcano or Mauna Kea. Be sure to pack hiking shoes, a light raincoat, and sunscreen, preferably with an SPF factor of 15 or better. The sun is fierce and can sunburn tender skin even on a cloudy day.

Check the Map of the Big Island. If you faced North, and symbolically cut the island in half in a North/South direction, you'd end up with the windward area of East Hawaii (Volcano, Hilo, Hamakua, and Waipio) on your right. In the center of the island you'd see two mountains, Mauna Kea and Mauna Loa. On your left would be West Hawaii, that is the Kohala-Kona Coast.

As in Spain, the rain falls mainly on the plain in East Hawaii. The heaviest downpours fall between October and April. Ka'u, the Southwest section of the island, tends to be dry, and three to five days may go by without rain. But even in Ka'u, you'll find microcosms of green tucked away in the interior valleys. Unlike many other vacation spots, any time of the year is a wonderful time to visit.

The island divides itself naturally into six diverse sections, with six different visual landscapes and vastly different climates. Hilo is the center of population in East Hawaii. Kailua is the center of population in West Hawaii. The local inhabitant of each town is firmly convinced that his little plot of terra firma is the best, the most desirable spot on the island. Ask a Hiloan, "How do you like Kona?" The answer invariably will be, "Oh, nice, but too hot!" Ask a Kona resident, "How do you like Hilo?" More likely than not, the answer will be a wrinkled nose and "Too much rain!" Waimea and the Volcano areas are high on the mountain, thus too cold for some, but as one retiree said: "No one could find fault with Kailua-Kona at a twelve hundred foot elevation. The weather's perfect!"

Climate in Hawaii is definitely a big plus. If you prefer cooler weather, the Volcano or upcountry Waimea is your bag, as the kids say. You can enjoy a fireplace, forty degree weather in the mornings, and grow strawberries and hydrangeas (huge, blue, cold-weather flowers) year round. Or if you enjoy the beach and water sports, swimming, surfing, snorkeling, and fishing "no ka oe!" (It's the best!)

Seasonal snow on the upper slopes of Mauna Kea makes it possible to ski, but it isn't easy, because of the high altitude and lack of facilities. The snow on Mauna Kea is excellent powder, but there is no ski-lift and transportation to the site must be done in a four-wheel drive vehicle. There is one ski guide service available.The generally balmy weather over most of the island makes outdoor exercise pleasant year round. This undoubtedly contributes to the fact that (and you might want to give this some serious thought) **Hawaii residents live longer than their counterparts in the other 49 states!** The pure fresh air, clean water, and generally pollution-free environment is remarkably healthful. Let's take a quick look at the Climate Chart that follows:

CLIMATE CHART

STATION	ELEVATION ABOVE S.L.	AVG. TEMP COOLEST MONTH	AVG. TEMP WARMEST MONTH	RECORD TEMP. LOW	RECORD TEMP HIGH	AVG. ANNUAL RAIN FALL (INCHES)
HILO AIRPT	30	71.2	75.9	63	94	128
VOLCANO	3970	57.6	63.2	37	85	101
NAALEHU	675	70.2	76.2	55	90	47
KAILUA-	30	72.1	77.3	54	93	25
PUAKO	5	73.1	79.8	52	98	10
WAIMEA	2670	61.3	66.8	34	90	31
HONOKAA	1070	67.6	75.5	N/A	N/A	86
MAUNA KEA	13796	31.3	42.5	11	66	20
SOURCE: STATE OF HAWAII DATA BOOK, TABLE 153, NOVEMBER 1991						

Understand, these aren't average temperatures, which can give a distorted impression, but average high and low readings. Not bad, wouldn't you say? But what about living costs? What about Hawaii being so expensive? What about jobs?

Cost of Living and Job Situation

If the crime-free environment, near perfect climate and breathtaking beauty of Hawaii makes you want to quit your job and hop on an airplane bound for the island - stop right there.

Nearly all jobs are to be found on Oahu, where living is very expensive. There the cost of housing, either to rent or to buy, is high. Very few people live on the outer islands and commute daily by air to work on Oahu, although the longest flight takes only fifty minutes. The cost of air travel and the possibility of sold-out flights make such a trip difficult for you to work fixed hours, or to keep appointments. For example, you can buy an air commuter coupon book of six tickets on sale that works out to spending $94 per day round trip. You can see why not many workers find that feasible.

The numbers of inter-island job commuters will undoubtedly increase in the next century. Perhaps large, stable ferry boats will ply the waters between the islands making such commutes viable, but, for now, **you need monthly retirement or other**

independent income to survive on the outer islands. However, the job picture is changing rapidly as new businesses locate here, and it may not be long before you could find job opportunities. For example, the Lanihau Shopping Center in Kailua-Kona is adding 50 new stores, with additional construction starting in Summer, 2000. When completed, this project will generate 600 new jobs.

To be sure, there are some entrepreneurial opportunities on Hawaii, usually connected with tourism. A few Snorkel Bobs or Deep-Sea Diving Daves have managed to survive. There are always some opportunities for professionals (doctors, lawyers, dentists, accountants, realtors, bankers) and for some blue-collar trades (construction workers, welders, fishermen).

However, the vast majority of jobs, since they are tourist oriented, are service jobs - (retail clerks, service station jockeys, hotel attendants, desk clerks, waiters, cocktail waitresses, and bartenders). They pay minimum wage. Also, there is a pervasive bias against hiring newcomers, as it is assumed from past experience that they don't remain in the islands very long and that, therefore, the employer will have the expense of retraining another employee too soon. True. It's extremely difficult to live in Hawaii on $5.25 an hour, or a dollar more with an increase in the minimum wage soon to be enacted.

Low wages force many to work two or even three jobs to make ends meet. When reality testing occurs, many who desperately want to remain in Hawaii, including many local people, simply can't do so when outgo regularly exceeds income. However, **if you have a minimum of $1,000 of independent income** (to support two adults), that income can be stretched in many ways, and supplemented, to make living in Hawaii very affordable. It boils down to knowing where to look for housing, where and how to shop to cut costs like the oldtimers do, and, in general, how to obtain real value for your dollar without sacrificing a comfortable lifestyle. We will show you how many people today are doing it.

WHAT'S IT LIKE?

Since where you decide to live is so important to your budget, maybe we better take a look at what's out there. Settle back, relax, and we'll take a quick armchair tour of the island. That way you'll gain instant knowledge of the different climates and terrain. Once you know what to look for, we can go house hunting!

There's just one thing. I'm afraid I'll have to take Pueo with us, because he'll have a purple fit if I go off and leave him home alone. He's not much trouble for a pet owl. (Owl?)

He's 10 years old. Just a baby in an owl's lifespan. Owls can live for more than fifty years. That's why the phrase "Wise old owl" came into being. I guess I've kinda gotten used to having him follow me around. In fact, sometimes he's been a big help. I've learned to rely on what he tells me because he's a Hawaiian owl. According to legend, Hawaiian owls never lie. But that's another story.

Before we start we'd better look again at our Map of Hawaii. This island is big! It's roughly 95 miles long (Upolu Point on the North to South Point), and 80 miles wide (Kapoho Point on the East to Keahole Point in the West). It's more than twice the size of the other Hawaiian islands.

If we drive around the island on the coastal road, we'll be covering about 225 miles. Since my home is at the Volcano, we might as well start our armchair tour right here, especially since this is one of the most interesting areas.

I want to give you an idea of each area, so that when you arrive, you'll already have in mind what you think will appeal to you. Of course, nothing I could say would really prepare you for the beauty of this island. But I'm not going to use superlatives. I'll leave that up to you!

East Hawaii

The Volcano and Puna

I can hear you saying it already. You mean people live on an active volcano? Or, what kind of crazy people would live near an active volcano? Surprise! The Volcano houses about 1,500 fulltime residents and about 150 vacationers. The cool climate, peace, and great beauty of the area make it a favorite get-away spot for weary city dwellers. There are actually five volcanoes on the island, the dormant volcano, Hualalai, above the village of Kailua-Kona; Kohala on the Northwest section; Mauna Kea, the tall "white mountain", Mauna Loa, the "long mountain", both of which occupy the center of the island, and Kilauea on the slopes of Mauna Loa. **Mauna Loa** and **Kilauea** are both active volcanoes, and it is this section of the island, located partly in the Puna District, that is commonly referred to as "The Volcano."

The Volcano is home to Volcanoes National Park, one of the most interesting and diverse parks in the National Park System, encompassing 344 square miles, taking in at its higher elevation Mauna Loa's firepit (Halemaumau crater), and at its lower elevation the seacoast of Puna.

Much has been written about the Volcano, but it needs to be experienced with all five senses to appreciate its diversity, its sheer power and awesome beauty. Occasionally, huge fountains of red lava approaching 1,700 feet high arc into the sky, and rivers of molten lava ooze into the sea, creating great clouds of steam as new land is formed. You can be impressed with pictures of an eruption, but nothing prepares you for the mighty amplification of a thousand lions roaring. You can hear it from miles away!

Right now a new island is visibly being formed off the Puna seacoast, named Loihi. This is truly the forest primeval, where the forces of creation and extinction have become a spectator sport.

High on the mountain volcanic ash (scree) has fallen, denuding trees and layering soil with new lava. Lower on the

13

slopes, forests thick with giant tree ferns, ohia trees, hundreds of different plants and exotic flowers and berries provide vivid contrast to the stark black lava fields. The high volcano landscape looks as if there could be a dinosaur peering out from behind the next tree. Jurassic Park could have been filmed here. When I mentioned that to Pueo, he gave a little screech and hid under the bumper of my 1988 yellow Mazda pick-up! (Actually, portions of "Jurassic Park" were filmed on the island of Kauai).

The climate tends to be chilly and wet at the Volcano, dipping into the forties early in the morning. Eerie mist and fog are common in early morning and evening, cloaking the forests, and inspiring drivers to turn on headlights.

The mists and fog of Kilauea provide the perfect backdrop for local legends and sightings of the Volcano Goddess Pele, who commonly takes the form of a beautiful young maiden when she is high on the mountain, and that of an old crone with streaming white hair and a little white dog beside her, when she wanders down to the seacoast.

For this reason, it's considered bad luck to refuse to give food upon request to an old woman along the seashore. She just might be Pele in disguise. Don't anger her or she'll trigger the volcano!

In Hawaiian lore, gods and goddesses could easily change form, sometimes appearing as a man or woman, or as a shark, bird, lizard, or other creature. The legends are fun to discover, but they are not to be taken lightly. They are part and parcel of island culture. Pueo has told me several local legends. He's a veritable fountain of information. For example, it's customary to leave offerings along the rim of Kilauea's Halemaumau Crater for the Goddess, which might take the form of fruit, flowers, or liquor. Pele is said to have a taste for gin, and occasionally bottles are hurled into the crater as an offering to the Goddess to appease her appetite. Pueo says he prefers Budweiser.

Going back to your inquiry - do people really live there? Indeed they do. The general consensus of opinion among the residents of Volcano is that they are in no more danger than the residents of Anchorage or Los Angeles, or of any other area which is exposed to natural disasters. In fact, they feel a lot safer living at Volcano than if they had to drive daily in any of America's large cities.

Kilauea's current eruption started in January 1983, and even though there have been many pauses in the flow of lava, scientists consider this a single, 17 year eruption. It has destroyed 181 housing units in Puna, but added about 500 acres of new land to the island.

The fact is that these volcanoes do not erupt with the explosive force of a Pinatubo or Mt. St. Helen's. They are saucer shaped shield volcanoes rather than cone volcanoes. Vents on their flanks relieve much of the pressure. They have been relatively benign in the modern area, attracting visitors, rather than repelling them.

Big Islanders welcome eruptions for the increase in tourism that results. Kilauea is known affectionately as the world's first "drive-in" volcano. The Hawaiian Volcano Observatory keeps a close watch on activity and has been doing so since 1919. You can even telephone the 24 hour Volcano hotline at (808) 985.6000 for eruption news, best viewing areas, and earthquake activity. Isn't that a gas?

For tourists, there is much to explore in the Park, ranging from the Chain of Craters, to the Thurston Lava Tube, the Observatory Museum with its displays and colored movies of past eruptions, the wonderful Volcano House with its incomparable view of Halemaumau firepit, sulphur banks and hot baths, bird parks, black sand beaches, trails to explore through the ohia forests. One day is not enough to see it all.

Do you prefer a cool climate? You'll find it here. Local residents have built homes throughout the area on beautifully wooded sites and enjoy the deep peace of the woods, broken only by birdcalls. A fireplace is a must. A light jacket, sweater, and jeans, are the uniform of the day. You'll find a couple of grocery stores, numerous bed and breadfasts, a small shopping village (Volcano Village), and the Volcano Golf and Country Club invites the public to play the course. (Your drive goes further at a 4,000 foot altitude!)

The Volcano/Puna area is rural and therefore not all of the homes have electricity. Those that are not hooked up to power lines have their own generators. Solar power is a new industry on the island and many homes are installing solar panels. Also, some homes depend on catchment water tanks which filter rainwater for bathing and washing clothes. This water is recycled to water gardens in dry areas. Wet areas, such as the Volcano, have ample rainfall to fill the tanks. Some residents prefer to drink bottled water.

In Volcano/Puna it is really necessary to distinguish between those homes that are at the 3,000 to 4,000 foot elevation, and those lower down on the Puna seacoast. In the higher elevation, you are in a fern forest. Down in Puna it is much drier, and the vegetation reflects a drier climate, with coconut palms lining the seashore.

C'mon Pueo, hop in the truck! We'll zip 32 miles South to Hilo in no time. As we descend down Hwy 11 to crescent-shaped Hilo Bay, the road is lined on both sides with giant tree ferns and stands of fragrant wild yellow and white ginger.

Hilo

If you decide to fly into East Hawaii, your first sight will be the little town of Hilo, population about 39,000, undoubtedly one of the prettiest, most charming towns in the world (when the sun shines!) It could be likened to Salem, Oregon, or perhaps Christchurch, New Zealand, with an Oriental twist. Hilo averages a whopping 132 inches of rain per year, and it's said often, only partly in jest, that Hiloans must have webbed feet. It seems sometimes that even the individual raindrops are outsize. But, Ah! The nighttime symphony of raindrops on the tin roofs of Hilo is nature's compensatory lullaby.

Since Hilo boasts an excellent deep-water harbor in its crescent-shaped bay, its development started early in the last century. It is the seat of local government. Only recently has West Hawaii become vocal in trying to obtain tax funds to be spent on roads and infrastructure in Kona-Kohala. Haole (Caucasian) newcomers have been mostly attracted to the sunny beach climate of West Hawaii. Hilo's population reflects the diverse polyglot racial strains of Hawaii - mostly a mixture of East and West (Japanese, Chinese, Filipino, Korean, Hawaiian, and Portuguese) and a more delightful group of responsible, friendly, and gentle people are not to be found anywhere.

The climate, although wet, tends to be comfortably cooler than in West Hawaii. Hilo's rains are warm, warm as the smiles and happy faces with which Hiloans habitually greet visitors. The incredible profusion of orchids, the exotic anthuriums and bird of paradise, the sweet plumeria, gardenias, and ginger growing wild by the side of the road, are unmatched. Hilo is simply beautiful. Who could forget the sight of a snow-capped mountain (Mauna Kea) tinged pink in the dawn's early light, reflected in the stillness of Hilo Bay?

Here rain can be a plus (you rarely have to water your yard and flowers), or it can have nuisance value (you'll probably want to keep light bulbs on in your closets to deter mildew). If you can tolerate damp weather, Hilo may be for you. It has a lot going for it.

Pueo says he's not going any farther without a Bud, so I guess we'll make a quick pit stop. Bossy little bird! Next on our Eastside journey is the Hamakua Coast. It'll take us about an hour to drive from Hilo to Honokaa, and then another fifteen miniutes to Waipio Valley.

Hamakua Coast

The Hamakua Coast is Hawaii's East border. Its climate is very comfortable and not quite as wet as Hilo. Rainfall is ample. Here fertile soil reaches across the eastern slope of its tallest mountain, Mauna Kea, to the eastern shore. Until recently, thousands of acres of sugar cane stretched for miles as far as the eye can see. The road is winding, around cliffs and down into steep valleys. Deep gorges are split by scenic waterfalls. After a rain, hundreds of waterfalls appear along the coast, and rainbows arch across the horizon.

Hamakua is populated by a series of little plantation towns as quaint and picturesque as their names: Papaikou, Pepeekeo,

Hakalau, Laupahoehoe, and Honokaa. Blink your eyes and you've passed the little towns. There are about 5,500 people living along the coast, but if you include the towns closer to Hilo, referred to as South Hilo, plus Laupahoehoe (North Hilo), that number jumps to nearly 12,000 residents. Population density is low.

The drive from Hilo to Honokaa is a visual feast. Gigantic palm trees, frangipani, African tulip trees with huge orange blossoms, and monkeypod, march down the deep gorges to the seashore. The bright golden wand of early morning light blessed the sugar cane fields, transforming them into shimmering waves of gold.

Hamakua is greener and wetter than West Hawaii, and offers magnificent ocean views. Papaikou, which is nearest to Hilo, or at the other end, Honokaa, which is a short 15 minute drive to Kamuela, are probably more desirable from the standpoint of convenient shopping. There are numerous homesites along the Coast affording spectacular views.

Pueo noticed that we were nearly out of gas. So we stopped for a tankful. All of a sudden he started sneezing and hiccuping. It happens every time he has a beer. Either he drinks it down too fast, or he's allergic. I told him from now on he'd better stick to Sprite. He said he didn't give a hoot, he's not giving up his Bud, and sulked all the way to Waipio.

Waipio Valley

We took a right turn off Highway 19 to the town of Honokaa, then a left on Mamane Street, continued driving for fifteen minutes until the road ends, and we're there. We walked to the lookout point overlooking the valley. Awesome.

Only a handful of people live in Waipio, (the "land of the falling waters") today, although a new resort is planned for the bluff overlooking the valley. One of the few remaining pristine refuges left virtually untouched by modern civilization, once seen, Waipio's fragile beauty is never-to-be-forgotten. It should be preserved and militantly guarded.

Thought by ancient Hawaiians to be the gateway to another life, steep walls shelter the deep valley floor, where today a few families still live and plant taro as did their forefathers. Hundreds of families lived in Waipio until the 1946 tidal wave swamped the valley floor. Today, living here is rugged indeed, without electricity or running water.

The haunting beauty of Waipio has inspired several melodic Hawaiian songs ("Hiilawe") which pay tribute to the giant waterfalls cascading eight hundred feet down the sides of the canyon. The view of the valley from the overlook is stunning, not to be missed, and inspires awe in tourist and resident alike. Time seems suspended here, offering a glimpse of the past and a vision of the future.

Most who see Waipio would like to see its beauty preserved, unspoiled by modern development of any kind. For this reason we haven't included information on basic housing costs for this area, and indeed, there are only a handful of properties on the market. No rentals except for a special little inn with a few rooms to let.

When we reached the junction of Highway 19 to turn right to Kamuela, I decided to backtrack a mile and turn into the landmark Tex's Drive-In for a steaming hot cup of coffee and a malasadas. (Portuguese doughnut without the hole). Pueo commented that I ought to lose 10 pounds and shouldn't be eating doughnuts. How rude. He was just trying to get back at me. I enjoyed that doughnut so much I decided to have two. Maybe he's right. I better start counting the calories. Why is it that I always feel remorseful **after** I gulp down the goodies and not before? The coffee was good, too. Let's hele on our way again. At this rate we should be in Kohala in an hour.

West Hawaii

North Kohala

We moseyed through Kamuela town and took Highway 250 to North Kohala. Big Islanders don't distinguish between North and South Kohala in everyday speech, referring to both sections

19

of the island simply as "Kohala". North Kohala's climate is very cool. Sweaters and a warm jacket are needed in winter months.

This windy, remote pastureland is believed to be the birthplace of King Kamehameha, the first Hawaiian king who united most of the islands under his rule in 1795 (except for Kauai island, the last holdout which entered the fold in 1824). Those were bloody battles, fought by King Kam's warriors against the ruling chiefs on each island. Rivers ran red with blood. Those old Hawaiians were huge men, between six and seven feet tall. Over the years, they intermarried with much shorter races. Today, the Hawaiian race is a much shorter composite. There are very few pure blooded natives left and few people speak the Hawaiian language, although there has been a renaissance of sorts lately in the schools.

North Kohala is rich in Hawaiian history. It is a leisurely 45 minute drive from Kamuela in Waimea to the little town of Hawi. The road winds and affords spectacular views through the whispering ironwood trees of the neighboring island of Maui and its extinct volcano Haleakala (the House of the Sun).

Pueo seemed to be in better spirits, and he entertained me with the legend of why the Hawaiians believed that the sun slept each night inside Haleakala crater. He said to tell you that if you come to visit, he'll tell you the story, too.

When we reached Hawi town, we turned right in the direction of Hilo, and in five minutes we reached its sister community of Kapaau. We couldn't resist a stop at Tropical Dreams, the local ice cream factory. Fresh fruit sorbets, homemade ice cream, macadamia nut and honey butters that are a 10. Free tastes! (Oh, well, I'll skip dinner to make up for it).

Quite a few homesteaders have recently built homes in Kohala overlooking the ocean and Maui. But for the most part, the area tends to be wild, windy, and remote (but beautiful.) There are numerous archeological digs and ancient Hawaiian heiaus or religious temples. The friendly population numbers only about 4,300 and there are few amenities.

Unless you're a bit of a hermit, year round living would be sort of like living in a remote Montana hamlet without the snow. However, if you enjoy going to bed with the chickens and getting up with the roosters, and your idea of entertainment is a Saturday night video, then this part of the island could be for you.

We were beginning to fade, Pueo and I, when we arrived back in Waimea. We decided to stay overnight, but couldn't find a hotel. We were lucky to find a room at the one bed and breakfast in the area - Kamuela's Mauna Kea View Bed and Breakfast. It had a queen size bed that was especially comfy. I preempted the bed, and Pueo perched on the window sill. He sleeps on one leg standing up, hunkers down, and pulls his feathers in around him. He's a cute little feller, which helps to make up for his sassy remarks, although I wouldn't tell him so!

Early in the morning he pounced on a yummy lizard for breakfast, (Ugh!) while I enjoyed my fruit and coffee. We were a little slow getting going again, but it was a gorgeous, sunny day as we sped through the green pastureland of Waimea.

Waimea

Waimea is upcountry. It is technically considered part of South Kohala. Its population numbers approximately 6,000 residents, but if you include the neighboring small villages of **Puako** and **Waikoloa,** that number jumps to over 9,000. Waimea is ranch country - home to Parker Ranch - the largest privately owned ranch (225,000 acres) in the United States. Parts of it resemble East Texas, green and hilly. Lower down on the slopes the climate is dry and you'll find cactus and tumbleweeds.

Upcountry is cool - downright cold in winter. Coats, jeans and sweaters, and a fire burning in the fireplace are necessary in winter, as the temperature is normally in the sixties during the day, but may drop down to the thirties and forties early in the morning. Yet you can drive down to the beach for a mid-day swim in a half hour.

Here we found wonderful vegetables and flowers grown in deep, black soil, July rodeos, and everybody's surname is either Lindsey, Purdy, or Spencer. When the Lindsey family gets together for a barbecue, there may be more than 1,000 family members present! The ranch and interlinked bloodlines have created bonds that have forged a strong, united community spirit.

We're driving through an area now that is more populated than what we've seen since Hilo. This area has recently acquired a new sophistication, with world-class restaurants and resorts opening to cater to a new breed of gentleman farmer and a spate of celebrities who vacation here. **Kamuela**, (the Hawaiian pronunciation of "Samuel" for Samuel Parker, the founder of Parker Ranch) is the town center, and offers adequate and interesting shopping facilities, as does the nearby **Village of Waikoloa.** From the standpoint of beauty, climate, and amenities, Waimea is a 9 on a scale of 1 - 10.

We didn't tarry long in Waikoloa because we had a lot of ground to cover. Pueo complained of a stomach ache. That lizard didn't agree with him. He made me promise to help him find a mouse for his dinner. I didn't tell him that I had just received a couple of those ultrasonic pest control devices and was hoping to get rid of all pests around the house. But I think it takes at least two weeks to be effective. Well, if we can't find a mouse, we'll surely find a mongoose out in the yard!

Our journey will soon be coming to an end. We're going to breeze through South Kohala, Kona, and Ka'u on our way home to Volcano.

South Kohala and Kona

The dry and sunny Kona Coast is host to the Big Island's new (and expensive) mega-resorts - the Mauna Kea Beach Hotel, Hilton Waikoloa Village. Mauna Lani Bay, the Ritz-Carlton, and the Prince has just been completed. Perched atop lava fields which have been groomed to perfection, they have been pruned, irrigated, and elegantly landscaped to a new standard of man-made beauty. Surrounded by magnificent championship golf courses, botanical gardens, and incredibly beautiful coastal beaches, their natural ocean vistas and radiant sunsets are beyond compare. Visitors from all over the world fly in to enjoy the healing, relaxing respite of a Kona vacation.

Those who can't afford the nightly rates commanded by the mega-resorts, alight in downtown Kailua-Kona. The climate in Kona during the day at sea level is warm year round, growing hot in the summer months. Nights are comfortably cool.

Until recently a sleepy little fishing village, **Kailua** springs to life in July and August with the annual billfishing tournament, and in October, with the world-famous Ironman Triathlon. Kailua today is busier, with much construction activity, but thus far has retained its small town charm.

Its ancient rock walls and lush slopes planted with coffee fields and macadamia nut trees are green and peaceful. You can smell the sweet plumeria flowers as you walk along the ocean on Alii Drive. Look up and you'll see the white "Love Boat " (S.S. Constitution or Independence) steaming out of the harbor. The local population is laid-back and friendly, and there is a wide variety of dining, shopping, and recreational activities for the modest pocketbook as well as the more affluent one.

But Kailua-Kona has become so popular, particularly in the winter season, and the cost of living relative to other sections of the island is so high, that knowledgeable persons with modest pocketbooks head for South Kona (Kona Paradise, also called "Pebble Beach"), H.O.V.E. (Hawaiian Ocean View Estates), and the small towns in the Ka'u District, Volcano, and Puna for bargains in housing, either to rent or to buy.

By this time Pueo was getting restless. He said he'd better hurry home to Volcano because he promised to be back for his girlfriend's birthday. I said, "Okay. Go on ahead. I can finish up this tour on my own." Pueo waved aloha, swooped away on the next updraft, circled lazily overhead once, then soared towards home. (Just before he took off, Pueo reminded me that he couldn't accompany me on my upcoming trips to Maui and Kauai because he had promised his friend Kimo to help him pick coffee, but he would catch up with me in Waikiki.)

The hills were green with coffee trees on my left, and the road edged a drop-off cliff five hundred feet above the ocean on my right as I headed South through Captain Cook towards Ka'u.

Ka'u

The great mountains of Mauna Kea and Mauna Loa separating East from West Hawaii are more than just a visual barrier here. By preventing the trade winds and rain-bearing clouds from reaching Ka'u, they have helped to create a very different landscape, and a sunny, dry climate. In some places it is what the Hawaiians called kekaha (desolate), a rough landscape of stunted grasses and trees growing from crumbly lava. At the higher elevations, or where there is adequate rainfall, the lushness of the tropics returns with forests of eucalyptus and lehua, and flowering fields of ginger and macadamia nut orchards.

Ka'u is truly old Hawaii even today, with the emphasis on relaxing under a huge banyan tree while savoring "shave ice", heading out to sea to snorkel or fish, picnicking at the beach, or tending a garden. Like Rip Van Winkle, this area is only just beginning to stir from its long sleep to enter the 21st century. **Here you'll find the picturesque little towns of HOVE (Hawaiian Ocean View Estates), Waiohinu, Naalehu, Punaluu, and Pahala.** This area is very sparsely populated, offers very comfortable climactic conditions, beautiful ocean and mountain views, and a low cost of living.

We've just completed our armchair tour of the island. Now that you are somewhat familiar with the terrain and characteristics of each section, let's see what's available in the way of housing.

HOUSING

Availability and Cost

The cost of living in Hawaii is intimately related to the cost of land. Since the Big Island is so large (4,038 square miles), it has more land to develop than the other islands. Development in West Hawaii has lagged behind that of East Hawaii because of the water shortage, but it is growing rapidly now that new water sources have been located. Demand for land is not as great as on

Oahu, because so few jobs are available at the present time. More jobs are expected to be created soon, as the area is growing. Until now this unemployment factor has served to hold down prices in many areas, and the recent recession and low mortgage interest rates have created the best buying or rental climate in decades.

There's no doubt that sale prices and rentals are highest on the West side of the island. Kohala boasts the multi-million dollar neighborhood of Puakea Bay with huge homes on individual ten acre parcels, some oceanfront. Further south are million dollar hillside ranches overlooking the ocean at Kohala Ranch, and the beautiful ten acre ranchettes at Waikii Ranch. Then there are the golf course developments around the Mauna Kea Beach Hotel, and in Keauhou Kona around the Kona Country Club. All very upscale and well publicized. **The inexpensive areas have generally been overlooked in the media.**

Prices have generally declined since the boom years of the 1980's, particularly in high-end housing (which in Hawaii is $500,000 plus.) Sale prices and rentals are highest in West Hawaii, in the immediate vicinity of Kailua-Kona, with Hilo next in line. **Cheaper housing is to be found in East Hawaii with bargains in Kau, Volcano, and Puna.** Housing in Hilo is less expensive than Kona, (all that rainfall), but it is much higher there now than ten years ago.

Housing availability is greatest in Kailua/Waikoloa and in Hilo/Puna, the two centers of population on the island, but there is ample inventory today to buy or to rent island-wide; enough to meet present demand. We'll be more specific later on.

Building

So far we've been talking to you about buying or renting, but what about building your own home? On the mainland the most economical method of acquiring housing is to find a lot and build. The same is true here. There are many parcels for sale all over the island, ranging from small 7,000 square foot lots, to large farms or ranches. If you have the confidence and expertise to act as your own contractor, you can save a bundle. For example, if you're willing to paint and clean up, you can build a no frills house today for approximately $52.00 per square foot, or $78,000 for a 1,500 square foot home.

For those who lack confidence or know-how, there are many building contractors who will do the job for you. A building cost of $130 per square foot including appliances, carpeting, and drapes, using a general contractor, would be considered high end, $100 would be moderate, and $80 would be low end. There is also package housing available, where you can do some of the construction yourself.

Lots in the immediate vicinity of Kona or Hilo are expensive, but a good sized (12,000 sq.ft.) lot in a rural area could be purchased for $12,000 to $20,000. When I say rural, I mean that there will be a local higher priced grocery store nearby, but you would want to do your major grocery shopping once or twice a week in the vicinity of Hilo, Kamuela, or Kailua-Kona. Wherever you locate you'll find one of these towns about an hour's drive away. We'll zero in on lot prices in each area.

Housing construction on the island can differ considerably from that on the mainland. Hawaii has such a temperate climate that single-wall construction is common. Insulation is not usually used. Windows are not solid glass panes, but are individual glass louvres that can be opened to let the breezes in.

Building a home off the ground is recommended for air circulation underneath the structure. Air conditioning is seldom included, nor is heat, (low power bills!) except that you might want a fireplace at a higher elevation Volcano or Waimea home in winter. Building an elevated home also makes it easy to spray bug spray on the foundations once a month to discourage happy Hawaiian bugs from invading your airspace. The environment is so healthy here that all living things thrive, including bugs, but they are easily controlled. Many visitors are amazed that we don't seem to have much of a mosquito or fly population. You can truly enjoy outdoor living. There are no snakes in Hawaii, nor venomous life-threatening pests.

Building a home with a wide roof overhang is practical. The idea is to shelter your interior airspace from the sun. The idea is

not to build a passive solar house which may be suitable for many areas on the mainland where you might want to let sunlight in with skylights and no roof overhang. If you do this in Hawaii, you will find that you've built a hothouse, and you and your family are the indoor plants! Also, in the Kona area, think twice about building at sea level unless you don't mind being bathed in perspiration. Look for an elevation close to 1,000 feet or more to keep your cool even in summer!

Renting

Most owners advertise in the classified section of both island newspapers. For East Hawaii, most of the ads are in the Hawaii Tribune Herald. West Hawaii owners advertise in West Hawaii Today. Best to look on Sundays. You can have a paper mailed to you by writing to:

Hawaii Tribune Herald
355 Kinoole St.
Hilo, Hawaii 96720
Phone (808) 935-6621

West Hawaii Today
75-5580 Kuakini Hwy.
Kailua-Kona, Hi. 96740
Phone (808) 329-9311

Volcano/Puna

Since you'll undoubtedly be renting for awhile, let's take a look now at rentals in the Volcano/Puna area. We'll take a look at the cost of existing homes and lots later. I don't want to swamp you with information too fast, too soon.

This is a rural area, so there are no condominiums available. At the higher elevations at the Volcano, there are probably less than 50 homes for rent. Inventory is low in this area.

Average Monthly Rentals

High Volcano

Studio $350-$400
1 bedroom $400-$450
2 bedroom $500-$600
3 bedroom $650-$750

Larger golf course homes are available for $1,000 to $1,250.

Puna-Seacoast

There are more than 50 but less than 100 homes available:

1 bedroom $400 - $475
2 bedroom $500 - $650
3 bedroom $700 - $800

Comment: You can find decent rental housing in this area which is not expensive. The weather tends to be a bit rainy and overcast, but the temperature is very comfortable. There are some pretty little towns on the main Highway 11 between Volcano and Hilo that offer magnificent mountain views - **Glenwood** and **Mountain View.** This is flower country. Orchids, anthuriums, and other exotic flowers are commonplace, but uncommonly beautiful.

Hilo

There are approximately 150 rentals available, from small condominiums to large homes, most with beautiful views of ocean, mountain, or both. Prices vary according to location and view, and whether furnished or unfurnished. The following prices are for unfurnished units. Expect to pay an additonal $100 per month for a furnished place.

Apartments and Condominiums

Studio bath $340 - $450
1 bedroom 1 bath $400 - $650
2 bedroom 1 bath $425 - $725
2 bedroom 2 bath $650 - $950
There are some luxury oceanfront units available from $800 to $1,200.

Houses

1 bedroom 1 bath $550 - $600
2 bedroom 2 bath $600 - $625
3 bedroom 2 bath $625 - $875

Comments: There's an ample supply of condos and apartments to choose from at fairly reasonable prices. Certainly costs are less than in West Hawaii. It might take a bit of legwork to find a newer dwelling. About 50% of Hilo's houses are **old** (30, 40, 50 years), so you might inquire how old the place is before going out to see it.

Hamakua Coast

This is a rural area and there are no apartments or condos for rent. There may be a few cottages or homes available. You'd have to look in both newspapers for possibilities. We were able to find only a 3 bedroom 2 bath home for $750 and a 2 bedroom 1 bath for $475. Your best bet if you want to live along the coast is to find a lot and build your own home, or buy an existing home.

North Kohala

To say that there is a dearth of rental housing in the area is an understatement. If you want isolation, then this is your area, but you'd most likely have to build or buy.

We found only an older 3 bedroom home in Hawi for rent for $475. Also, there was a cabin to sublet for six months - but only to a cat lover and vegetarian! There are several ohana houses in the area (See Ohana Housing) and you might be able to find the top or bottom of an existing home to rent by watching the newspaper ads.

To RECAP what we've seen so far regarding renting: the Volcano (high elevation) has a few homes for rent, the lower Puna seacoast has a super inventory of inexpensive houses, Hilo has a large number of houses, apartments and condominiums that are reasonable. Scratch Hamakua Coast, Waipio, and North Kohala. Very low inventory there.

Waimea

There are very few apartments or condos to rent in Waimea. There are a few cottages, and about two dozen homes to rent. A cottage rents for $550 - $750. A larger home of 3 bedrooms and 2 baths rents for $750 - $1,200. The majority of homes are between $900 and $1,100. Rents are higher here than on the East side.

In the **Village of Waikoloa**, about a 20 minute drive south of Kamuela, we found a delightful community with ocean view surrounding a golf course. Here there are probably another two dozen homes for rent. These are newer homes (one to seven years old). Average monthly rentals are $1,000 to $1,300.

We did strike pay dirt with condos in **Waikoloa**. There are easily 40 condos for rent, mostly 2 bedroom 2 bath, ranging from $575 to $650 monthly. Not bad for a new, golf course, ocean view community.

South Kohala and Kona

Inventory varies greatly from winter to summer. The busy winter season extends from January through April when rentals are scarce. Other than winter, there are probably 100 condos, and 100 homes for rent in the immediate vicinity of Kailua.

Condominiums

Studio bath	$350 - $550
1 bedroom bath	$550 - $650
2 bedroom bath	$650 - $700
2 bedroom 2 bath	$800 - $975

Houses

3 bedrooms 2 baths $900 - $1,200
Larger homes $1,400 - $2,000 and up.
(Larger homes comprise those over 2,000 sq.ft.).

Rents are a great deal higher on the West side of the island, except for condo rentals in Waikoloa.

South Kona, Kona Paradise (Pebble Beach)

Because this subdivision is an hour's drive south of Kailua, a 3 bedroom 2 bath home rents for $650 - $850. There are about 10 homes available here.

Ka'u

There are no condominiums or apartments in this area.

Houses

In HOVE (**Hawaiian Ocean View Estates)**, there are approximately 50 homes to rent ranging from a 1 bedroom for $450 to a 3 bedroom 3 bath for $575. In **Discovery Harbor,** a lovely subdivision built around a golf course with ocean view, a 3 bedroom 2 bath home rents for $575 and there are a dozen available. There are a few houses for rent in the little country towns in the district. It's clear that this is bargain country.

To RECAP what we've seen so far:

In **East Hawaii** the high elevation Volcano has a few houses available, the lower Puna Seacoast has a super inventory of inexpensive homes, Hilo has an ample supply of inexpensive apartments, condos, and houses that are reasonable. There's very little to be found on the Hamakua Coast, Waipio, and North Kohala.

In **West Hawaii**, Waimea's cottages and houses command high rentals. Waikoloa has many inexpensive condos, South Kohala and Kona rentals are highest, but **South Kona and Ka'u offer terrific, very inexpensive house rentals.**

Ohana Housing

Ohana housing is very popular in Hilo and in East Hawaii. "Ohana" is the Hawaiian word for family. Ohana zoning was originally passed by the State Legislature as a way to let residents build a second home on their lots to house family members such as aged parents, or adult sons and daughters who could not afford to buy a home in the marketplace.

As it stands now, there is no minimum lot size requirement. Since the law is difficult to enforce (that only family members occupy the second home), you will find many ohana homes offered for rent to the general public. Kona's Republican representatives are attempting to tighten up zoning regulations to require that (1) the lot be at least 10,000 square feet in size (2) the home to be built only one story high (3) 25 foot sideyard setback (4) one person to be limited to one application in any two year period. You can see how developers could have a field day with ohana housing, being able to build two homes on one lot, resulting in overburdened streets and sewers. As we go to press these new restrictions have received only preliminary approval by the County Planning Committee. A majority are in favor of the new restrictions.

Buying Homes and Lots

If you decide that you'd be more interested in buying an existing home or lot, your best bet is to contact a reputable, licensed realtor. We recommend as honest, knowledgeable, and reliable:

Roger Hibline
Action Team Realty
P. O. Box 2019
Kailua-Kona, Hi. 96745
Phone: 808.329.8626

Alice Tredway
Alice Tredway Realty
75-5995 Kuakini Hwy. Ste. 123,
Kailua-Kona, Hi. 96740
Phone 808.329.1163

One of the best things about buying property in Hawaii is that once you have your deed and it's recorded, you own it! In some foreign countries, just because you have a deed, and you **think** you own the property, you may later find that someone else owns it, and all you have is a worthless piece of paper! Also, even if your evidence of title is genuine, in foreign countries there is rarely bank mortgage financing available and you're expected to pay cash for your purchase.

The property descriptions given here were compiled from many sources. Note that the prices mentioned are **asking** prices, not sales prices, and are negotiable. These are quoted to give you a general picture of the housing market. Recognizing that markets change, you'll need an up-to-date analysis of comparable sales prices. Should you become interested in buying, you'd want to contact a competent realtor who can do the analysis for you.

I told Pueo that you were interested in the information we'd given you so far on renting, but you also wanted to know the availability and cost of existing homes and lots for sale here.

Being a naturally nosy owl, he said he'd be point man, fly out to see what he could find, and report back to me, since he and Kimo wouldn't start picking coffee for another week. Here's what we compiled:

East Hawaii

Volcano and Puna

We found about 400 homes offered for sale in this area. There are many vacant lots for purchase, but no condominiums. Homes tend to be newer than in Hilo. If you were interested in an anthurium or orchid flower farm, you would be looking for one in the higher elevation Volcano area down to Hilo, rather than in Puna.

At the higher elevations Pueo found a few residential subdivisions (Mauna Loa Estates, Fern Forest, Fern Acres, Eden Roc, and Royal Hawaiian Estates). He said that there are approximately 40 homes offered for sale at the higher elevations. He wanted to know what you'd be interested in, and I told him to report back on the size of the house and lot, number of bedrooms and baths, and the price asked. This is what he learned: In **Fern Forest** and **Fern Acres**, subdivisions built right on green wooded sites, lot sizes are typically 2 or 3 acres. Typical offerings are:

Bed/bath	Living Area	Lot Size	Price
3/2	1,320 sq.ft	2 Acres	$75,000
5/2.5	2,304 sq.ft	2 Acres	$125,900

In **Volcano Village**, homes built near a little shopping center:

Bed/bath	Living Area	Lot Size	Price
1/1	852 sq.ft.	15,786sq.ft.	$115,000
3/2	1,288 sq ft.	1 Acre	$189,000

34

In **Mountain View,** a lovely area with a beautiful view near Hilo:

2/2	864 sq.ft	8,260sqft	.$79,000
3/2	1,140 sq.ft	8,340sqft	$99,500
3/2	1,323 sq.ft	8,346sqft	$119,000

In **Glenwood**, another lovely area, there are more affordable homes ranging from $79,500 to $110,000 for homes that are roughly 1,000 sqft. gross living area on a 10,000 sqft. lot.

I thanked Pueo for his help and sent him flying off to Puna. We learned that the Puna seacoast is studded with affordable homes. On the beach you would find subdivisions such as **Kapoho Beach** Lots and **Nanawale Estates**. In this area you would want to make a thorough investigation as to whether the area is on a rift zone of the volcano, in which case it could be too risky to build or buy unless you were able to obtain insurance. Your ability to obtain homeowner's insurance is **key** as to whether or not the home is considered at risk. If so, you may find it difficult to obtain insurance, and/or you may have to pay more for it.

Near Keaau town we found the subdivision of **Hawaiian Paradise Park**, where many lovely homes have been built. Prices in HPP range from $85,000 to $200,000 depending on size. A new home of approximately 1,300 square feet on an acre would run around $150,000. Another popular subdivision with similar pricing is **Orchid Land Estates**.

Hilo

Unlike Volcano and Puna, **Hilo's** homes are connected to city water and power. Asking prices here are roughly $80,000 to $100,000 higher, with homes close in commanding higher prices per square foot. There are approximately 190 homes for sale.

Prices range on average from $150,000 to $200,000. A typical newer home might be a 3 bedroom 2 bath 1,290 square feet gross living area, on a lot of 10,000 square feet, with an asking price of $189,000 to $199,000.

Some of the popular subdivisions are **Puainako, Waiakea**,and **Kaumana**. Many newer homes with beautiful views have been built on the mountain slope overlooking Hilo Bay. There are prestige homes offered for sale also, in areas such as **Sunset Ridge** - larger homes with an asking price of $230,000 up.

Many of Hilo's homes are beautifully landscaped with exquisite orchid gardens, but the homes are old. Probably 50% of homes on the market here are 40 to 60 years old. Owners attempt to sell these homes "as is", thereby disclaiming responsibility for repairs. Unless the buyer is a handyman, this can be a can of worms. Also, many of these older homes have had additions built without proper building permits which may become a problem for the buyer. Buyers should obtain full disclosure from the seller. If the seller is unwilling to do so, makes an excuse, or asks the buyer to do his own investigation, this should raise a red flag.

For obvious reasons, the buyer should not be asked to do his own investigation. There may be underlying defects that the owner may or may not know about, but that may not be apparent upon inspection. If you are tempted to buy an older home in Hilo, it would be prudent for you to do so through a competent real estate attorney. We recommend:

> **Steven B. Dixon, Attorney**
> **68-1760 Nawili Place**
> **Waikoloa, Hi. 96738**
> **Phone: 808.883.8377**

While any attorney must charge a fee for his time, the fee that you pay him for avoiding a gross mistake is often worth many times his fee. You could save a bundle by submitting the contract to Steve before signing, or write into the contract that it is subject to his approval.

Hilo is a delightful town in which to live. It just takes a little leg work to find the right place. Renting a house or condo for six months while you look around is highly advisable. You'll find most people in this area to be extremely kind, honest, gentle, and friendly.

Condominiums

At any given time Hilo offers about 100 condominiums for sale. Some waterfront condos along the Bayshore Drive are leasehold. (You don't own the land). If you should become interested in a leasehold property, it's advisable to discuss this with an attorney before proceeding so that you fully understand what you're getting into. Leasehold condos are priced lower, of course, than the fee simple ones (you own the land).

Some of the condos in Hilo have breathtaking mountain and/or ocean views. The majority are modestly priced compared to condos in West Hawaii, Maui, or Oahu. For example, a 3 bedroom 2 bath condo near the university, fee simple, with a floor area of 1,216 square feet is priced at $128,000. Prices range from $29,000 for a leasehold studio to $325,000 for an oceanfront, fee simple penthouse of 1,600 square feet. **Retirees should be able to find a great, affordable condo with terrific mountain and ocean views here!**

Lots

Hilo has at any given time about 100 lots offered for sale. Prices are higher than in Volcano/Puna and Kau, but less than in West Hawaii. In Waiakea, an old established neighborhood, lots of 10,000 - 15,000 square feet are selling for $95,000 to $100,000. In Puainako, a newer subdivision with better views, sellers are asking and getting $100,000 to $115,000 for 15,000 square feet lots. In upscale Sunrise Estates, 1 to 1.5 acres commands $100,000 to $130,000. Kaumana offers smaller lots of 7,500 square feet for $37,500 - $42,500, and larger parcels of 18,000 to 22,000 square feet at prices ranging up to $169,000.

Hamakua

There are no condos here. This is where you'd look if you were interested in a small farm or ranch. Since Hamakua is so sparsely populated, there are not many homes offered for sale - a total of only 44 from the little town of Honomu through Honokaa. Since Hamakua Sugar is closing down, that company is offering parcels of sugar land for sale. However, the County may be appropriating hundreds of acres of land in lieu of back taxes. In any case, there should be a great deal of farmland available. Soil is deep and rich in Hamakua with ample rainfall - a farmer's dream! The climate is delightful, streams and waterfalls abound, and mountain and ocean views are spectacular. There are a few homes offered for sale along the coast in a price range of $150,000 to $200,000. These homes typically have a gross living area of 1,200 square feet on lot sizes of 10,000 to 12,000 square feet. The least expensive small home offered is priced at $78,000. More homes are clustered in Honokaa with asking prices of $120,000 to $199,000. Since there are so few homes available in this area, if you wanted to relocate here, your best bet would be to buy a lot and build.

Lots

There are close to 200 lots offered for sale along the Hamakua Coast, excluding parcels that may be offered by the Hamakua Sugar Co. Many of these are small macadamia nut orchards or flower farms. Smaller house lots of 8,000 to 10,000 square feet seem to be clustered near Hilo and near Honokaa. Between these two towns most of the parcels are zoned Agricultural 10 to 20 Acres, and there are many large parcels offered for sale.

Near Hilo, in a subdivision called **Nani Malio**, lots slightly over 8,000 square feet are being offered at $77,000 to $81,000. This is a new subdivision with underground utilities, which is a rarity on the island. Near the town of Honokaa, we found a newer subdivision also with underground utilities and a great ocean view where lots of about 10,000 square feet are selling for $60,000 to $80,000.

An important consideration to anyone thinking of purchasing one of the beautiful agricultural parcels of land along the coast is whether utilities such as telephone and electric are hooked up to the property. If not, how much would it cost to connect?

Here are some examples of larger acreages to be found along the coast that are offered for sale:

14. Acres	$239,000	
11.7 Acres	$935,000	(oceanfront)
1.5 Acres	$370,000	(includes 4 homes)
10.2 Acres	$300,000	
4.97 Acres	$289,000	
7.28 Acres	$219,000	
12.35 Acres	$495,000	
17.71 Acres	$225,000	
38.7 Acres	$1,950,000	

Pueo had squeaked that he'd take the 38 acre parcel. When I pointed out what the taxes would be, he said he'd pass.

West Hawaii

North Kohala

There are no condos in this area. Excluding the very expensive subdivisions of Puakea Bay and Kohala Ranch, there are only ten properties being advertised for sale. Several are ohana (See Chapter 4 - Ohana Housing), with rental units downstairs or upstairs. Again, this is country, and the lot sizes are quite large - 10,000 to 15,000 square feet. Several older homes (30 to 40 years old) are advertised. One asking price is $165,000 for a 1,300 square foot home on a 15,000 square foot lot. A newer, larger home on a 15,000 square foot lot is advertised at $199,000. There's not much to choose from in this area in the way of existing homes. Best bet is to buy a lot and build, but since the lots advertised are so large your cost going in may be too high.

Lots

There are only about 40 vacant lots being advertised for sale in this area. Several are large parcels of 8, 9, or 10 acres. Here you might find a larger lot of 17,000 square feet convenient to schools and shopping with a price tag of $70,000. There are some 1-5 acres lots available at **Maliu Ridge** with beautiful ocean views. These lots have price tags of $150,000 for an acre, less for larger lots. Five years ago an acre lot sold for $79,500 to $89,500. Historically, appreciation for Hawaii fee simple land has been extremely rapid due to its scarcity and high demand. In 1997, with worldwide disinflation, it's anybody's guess as to what will happen to land prices in the future.

Waimea

Homes here are electrified and have piped water. Those familiar with Waimea divide it into "wet-side" and "dry-side", with the climate growing progressively wetter as you drive Northeast from Kamuela, and drier as you descend Southwest into South Kohala and the beaches. Homes in South Kohala and Puako on the ocean tend to be very expensive, and homes in Waikoloa and in the vicinity of Kamuela are moderately priced except for "Nob Hill" and Mokuloa Subdivision. We have deliberately omitted the very high priced subdivisions of Mauna Kea Fairways and Kohala-By-The-Sea.

In the Kamuela area look for subdivisions such as **Kamuela Meadows, Puu Nani, Waimea Homesteads, Pleasant Acres, and Kamuela Highlands**. Here you'll find attractive homes in a price range of $150,000 to $200,000. There are approximately 25 of these homes on the market.

Probably some of the better buys for newer homes on the island are to be found in **Waikoloa Village**. These are newer homes, most under seven years old, in a price range of $180,000 to $250,000. There are approximately 100 homes to choose from. This is a golf course community, with ocean view, and membership in the Waikoloa Country Club is usually included in the purchase.

Condominiums

There are very few in Kamuela and in the nearby Kawaihae area offered for sale - only ten. These are not very appealing, being either overpriced or not very attractive.

In **Waikoloa Village**, on the other hand, there are nearly 120 condos on the market that are very attractive and affordably priced. **Condo bargain hunters, look here!** Most of these units are clustered around a golf course and have beautiful ocean views as well! You should be able to purchase a spacious, fee simple 2 bedroom 2 bath 800 square foot unit for $100,000 to $120,000. Expect to pay slightly more for a larger unit.

Lots

In Waimea there are presently about forty lots being marketed.

The low end of the market is to be found in **Kamuela Lakeland**, where you might pay about $80,000 for a 10,000 square foot lot. A moderate price for this area would be found in **Puu Nani Subdivision**, where the price range is $100,000 to $130,000 for a 12,000 square foot lot. The high end for lots close to Kamuela town is **Mokuloa Subdivision**, where the price range is $169,000 to $245,000 for lots of 1 acre or more.

Again, more selection and better priced lots are to be found in **Waikoloa**. There are currently about 40 lots offered for sale here. Lot sizes range from 10,000 to 18,000 square feet, and prices range from $62,000 to $115,000. Proximity and view of the golf course and ocean are pricing factors.

South Kohala and Kona

Omitting the very expensive beach and golf course homes, there are nearly 400 homes offered for sale in the vicinity of

Kailua - a nice inventory. However, you'll find almost none under $150,000 and very few under $200,000. The vast majority of homes range between $200,000 and $500,000. Much cheaper housing is to be found in South Kona near the Ka'u border, and in the District of Ka'u.

Low end neighborhoods are **Kona Coastview, Harbor View, Kona Highlands,** and **Queen Liliuokalani Village**. Here you'll find homes ranging from $150,000 to $200,000.

Middle end neighborhoods, where homes range from $200,000 to $300,000 are: **Kona Palisades, Kilohana and Komohana Kai, Kailua View Estates,** and **Kuakini Makai.**

High end neighborhoods ($300,000 homes and up) are: **Kaloko Mauka, Hualalai Farms, Keopu Heights, Kona Heavens, Kona Orchards, Kona Hills Estates, Sunset,** and **Kona Bay.**

On your way south to Captain Cook, you'll find homes in the $200,000 to $300,000 range. In South Kona, about an hour's drive from Kailua village, at a subdivision called **Kona Paradise,** you'll find newer, truly affordable homes built on a hillside with fantastic ocean views. There are about a dozen for sale, ranging from $125,000 to $200,000.

Condominiums

There are roughly about 600 condos for sale in the vicinity of Kailua, with prices ranging from $40,000 up for a studio, $60,000 to $120,000 for a 1 bedroom, and $120,000 up for a 2 bedroom. Prices vary as to whether they are leasehold or fee, and how near they are to the ocean, with oceanfront units being more expensive. There are some moderately priced condos on the hillside with outstanding ocean views. **While Kona home prices may be out of reach for many retirees, Kona condos are not.**

Lots

There are approximately 300 lots available for sale in the Kailua area, but a buildable, affordable lot has become as scarce as hen's teeth. The vast majority of house lots are over $100,000. There are a few 7,000 square foot lots available in Harborview with an asking price of $79,000. In the popular neighborhood of Kona Palisades, 10,000 to 12,000 square feet lots range from $95,000 - $120,000.

Again, the most affordable building lots are to be found in South Kona, at **Kona Paradise, or "Pebble Beach"**. There are about 20 lots available ranging from $39,500 to $70,000. Most of these are about 7,500 square feet and have a tremendous ocean view.

Ka'u

This is a rural area and there are no condominiums. This area is the least developed and offers the least expensive homes for sale on the island.

In Hawaiian Ocean View Estates, currently there are about 70 newer homes for sale within a price range of $75,000 to $130,000. A handful are higher priced on 3 acre lots - the **Ranchos.** The majority of homes are on acre lots. All use water catchment tanks with filters. Homes are valued higher if they are close to the shopping center, close to the main highway, and if they have electrical connection to the property or nearby. There is no cable TV in this area. Residents use satellite dishes for program reception.

In **Discovery Harbor**, a lovely golf course community in Waiohinu, there are about 10 homes for sale clustered around the course, in a price range of $150,000 to $200,000. These homes, in addition to the golf course vista, have spectacular ocean views.

As you drive through the little towns of **Waiohinu, Naalehu, and Pahala,** you'll find very few homes for sale. Since jobs have been lost in the sugar industry, there may be more homes for sale in this area soon. Look around **Punaluu,** and you may find a few homes for sale within walking distance of the lovely black sand beach. This area is a sleeper, as the Sea Mountain Golf Resort has just been sold and the new corporate owner has well conceived and designed development plans.

Lots

There are nearly six hundred lots on the market for sale in **Hawaiian Ocean View Estates**. Most are one acre parcels and asking prices range from $6,000 - $12,000. The larger 3 acre parcels in the **Ranchos** range from $20,000 to $40,000.

In the **Mark Twain Subdivision** in Naalehu, there are approximately 65 larger lots available between $15,000 - $30,000.

In **Discovery Harbor** in Punaluu, there are nearly 60 lots for sale between $30,000 - $60,000 for lots of approximately 13,000 to 16,000 square feet. These have lovely golf course and ocean views, (and a nearly perfect climate.)

Most of the other lots in the area are scattered about the countryside and not too easy to locate. Directions are commonly given by place markers - "The blue house behind the yellow house next to the big rock by the banyan tree four telephone poles from the main road." This can be somewhat disconcerting to those used to a grid map, but it just adds to the general sense of adventure and countryside charm. Fortunately, if you get lost and have to ask directions, the locals are extremely hospitable and helpful.

RECAP: We've seen that the cost of existing homes and lots are highest in West Hawaii, South Kohala, and in Kona, with Hilo and Waimea vying for the dubious distinction of second place. **Much cheaper housing is to be found in South Kona near the Ka'u border, in Volcano/Puna, and bargains in Ka'u.** Here the cost of living is amazingly low, if you're willing to be flexible, and not buy all of your food at retail prices, but buy at the farmer's markets, grow a few items, and buy in bulk at the "off-price" giant discount houses.

Hawaii has seen its worst economic recession commencing with the Gulf War in 1992 and continuing on through the deccade of the 1990's. Real estate prices have dropped, then remained stagnant. However, there have been increased sales and rental activity since October, 1998, but we have yet to see any measurable increase in prices as of the beginning of 2000.

Now that we know what's going on in the housing market, let's take an in depth look at the cost of food, transportation, clothing, and utilities, to see how people are living well here on a modest income.

OTHER COST OF LIVING FACTORS

Food

It is well-known that retail prices of imported foodstuffs in the local supermarkets are shockingly high to mainlanders, and they wonder how we can afford to live here and pay such prices. The answer is - we don't buy **all** of our food retail, and not all of our food is imported. Hawaii is a breadbasket of delicious food.

Fruit

Hawaii's soil is so rich in nutrients; bright sunlight and rainfall alternate daily, and the result is a year round cornucopia of fruits and vegetables. Although papayas may sell for $.58 to $.78 per pound, bananas for $.68 per pound, and mangoes for a whopping $3.50 per pound in the supermarkets, many island yards have these fruits growing in abundance, ripe for picking. Breadfruit, passion fruit, limes, lemons, oranges, and grapefruit grow rapidly. Many islanders stroll out in the yard and pick breakfast off the trees. And avocadoes - Kona avos are huge, buttery, and so plentiful in some areas that they roll down the streets.

Fish

The seas are teeming with delicious white meat fish - bonefish (ono), mahimahi (dolphin), yellowfin and bluefin tuna (ahi and aku), swordfish or marlin (kojiki), shark, as well as a variety of shellfish. Fish is expensive in the stores, but if you have any fishing skills at all, you can try your hand at shoreline or pier fishing at the numerous beach parks, or do as the Hawaiians do, go out in an outrigger or dinghy.

If you're not inclined to fish yourself, make friends with the friendly local fishermen (easy to do), and they'll sell you fish at greatly reduced prices. Or - go to the Suisan fishmarket in Hilo early in the morning and put in a bid for a fish and freeze it. If you're in Kona go to the ice house at Honokawai Harbor at sunset and buy fish directly from the fishermen. Fish filets don't have to be expensive unless you buy at retail prices. (There is more than one way to skin a cat - fish, that is).

Additional sources: **Kona Cold Lobster** (wholesale and retail) phone 329-4332. **Uwajima Fishery**, phone 329-8480.

Vegetables

A vegetable garden consisting of squash, corn, and cherry tomatoes is easily grown. Again, you can pick your own vegetables. The biggest problem is scaring pests away, such as birds or mongoose. Here your cat or dog is your biggest ally. But again, if you don't want to become a part- time gardener, no big t'ing, as the locals say.

Fresh air farmer's markets are held several times every week in Hilo and Kona, where a superior variety of fresh vegetables and fruits are to be found at prices 30%-40% less than supermarket prices. Many locals go once a week just to load up on wonderful, fresh vegetables - lettuce, green beans, corn, squash, tomatoes and onions. Papayas sell typically three or four for a dollar.

Waimea, particularly, is noted for its superior vegetables. As you drive on Hwy 19 through the little town of Kamuela, stop at the **Vegetable Stop** on the mauka (mountain) side of the road just before the Kamamalu Street light. As you drive through Kamuela look for roadside signs that say "Fresh Strawberries". These are juicy and sweet. You can pick up fresh fruits and vegetables from numerous roadside stands around the island.

Additional Sources:
Seaweed Products
Hawaiian Sea Farms
Ask for Roy
Phone 329-5468

Try the **Farmer's Market** in Kailua. They have local and organic produce, bulk herbs, grains, and beans and low prices on avocados, bananas, and papayas. Of course if you don't choose to live in a condo, you'd want to grow your own papayas. All you have to do is scoop out the seeds and plant them. You don't even have to sprout the seeds, unless you want to grow a special variety. Banana trees are equally easy to grow.

Bread

Holsum/Orowheat Co. has a bakery in Hilo at 306 Kamehameha Ave. and in Kona at 74-5599 Alapa St., in the old Industrial Area, that sells marvelous day-old loaves and pastries at huge discounts. Although you may pay $3.50 for a loaf of bread at the supermarket, you can buy it here for $1.49. And, they give an additional 10% senior citizen discount. If you object to day-old bakery goods, go there on Wednesdays and you can get huge discounts on freshly baked goods. For example, bread sells for $1.65 per loaf. Also, if your purchase is $5.00 or more, they'll throw in a free loaf of bread. So - if you load up on crackers, hamburger and hot dog buns, you'll get a freebie!

Milk

I don't know what the cows in Hawaii are eating, but their milk is the richest ever. Excelsior and S & S Dairies in Naalehu, and Meadow Gold Co.in Hilo sell all they can produce. Unfortunately, their prices are higher than imported mainland milk! Why? They claim it's higher because they don't produce powdered milk, cheese and butter, so they're ineligible for federal subsidies, and any extra fodder has to be imported from the mainland. Why don't they produce cheese and butter? Who knows - speculation - maybe they prefer the higher prices?

Years ago, small groups could go to the dairies and buy milk at a discount. Or, you could buy milk directly from a small farmer. No more. Today, State Board of Health regulations have discouraged such sales. The most economical milk purchases are of powdered milk in the supermarket. $8.89 will purchase 12 one quart envelopes, which works out to $.74 per quart. Not bad. Coconut milk, of course, is readily available, but fattening. Just knock down some coconuts, peel the husks, (easier said than done), drill a hole in the shell, and insert a straw.

Eggs, Honey, Chicken and Specialty   **Cheeses**

May be purchased directly from local farmers at a discount.

Sources:

> **Panewa Egg Farm (Hilo)**   **959-6511**
> **Hawaiian Fresh Egg Farm**   **882-7931**
> **Honey Co-op (Walter Patton) 964-1046**

Also try **Big Island Eggs** - North Kohala and Kamuela - Phone 889-5976. They sell chicken and turkey, sausages, bagels and juices in bulk at wholesale.

Goat Cheese

Kuokoa Farms Kurtistown, HI.   966-7792

Feta Cheese

Island Dairy Ahualoa, HI.   775-2284

(This is a cheese of Greek origin. They are located opposite Honokaa on the Hamakua Coast. Island Dairy is making its own feta cheese and selling it statewide. Bahman Sadeghi, originally from Iran, has created his own niche in the dairy market)

Meat - Poultry, Beef, Pork

Much poultry is grown on the island and the price of chicken and turkey in the supermarkets is not particularly high. For example, frozen chicken legs sell for $.70 per pound, and thighs for $.77 per pound, not much higher than West Coast prices.

Nevertheless, you can purchase directly from the local poultry farms for even more savings.

Kona Poultry Farm
June Nakamoto................Phone 322-3161.

Fortunately, **Parker Ranch**, which raises more Hereford cattle than any other ranch in the world, sprawls across Waimea. Parker Ranch beef is outstanding. Their 90% lean hamburger meat cooks up into the tastiest hamburger you've ever had. For a special lunch treat, try the Parker Ranch Grill (formerly The Broiler) at the Parker Ranch Center, now under Huggo's management, phone 808.887.2624.

You can buy Parker ranch beef from the Kamuela Meat Market. This is a little hole in the wall and is not easy to find. In the Parker Ranch Shopping Center go around to the back of the Center and look for it next to the Sure-Save unloading ramp. Phone 885-4601. They're closed on Sun. and Mon. Open weekdays in the afternoon from 2 - 5:00 p.m., and Sat. from 9 a.m. to 1 p.m. Prices are great!

Here's a sample price list:

Bacon	12 oz	1.35
Sliced Beef (BBQ)	lb	3.12
Seasoned Beef	12 oz	3.10
Belly Pork mainland	lb	2.09
BBQ Sauce	qt	1.85
Boneless Stew	lb	2.32
Brisket Stew	lb	1.62
Chuck Roast	lb	1.89
Ground Beef (75/25)	lb	1.70
Ground Beef (90/10)	lb	2.54
Pork Steaks	lb	2.19
Sirloin Steak.	lb	3.02
T-Bone Steak	lb	4.05

I've abbreviated the list. They have many more cuts of steak, pork, and chicken for sale at reasonable prices. It's true that Parker Ranch beef is range fed, not corn fed beef, but the meat is as fresh as can be, tender, and flavorful.

KTA Supermarket is making a real effort to include locally grown produce, poultry, and pork on their shelves and has recently started to do so under the **Mountain Apple** label. Look for this label. Since there are no import costs, these products should sell for less than the mainland imports. For example, they are selling 90% lean ground beef for $2.19 per pound.

Miscellaneous: Soap powder, Cleaning solutions, Paper towels, Toilet paper, Et al.

These are best bought weekly in bulk from the discount houses Costco, K-Mart and Wal-Mart in Kona, Cost-U-Less and Wal Mart in Hilo. It is generally believed by mainlanders that the cost of transportation and/or extra labor in handling goods has been responsible for high import product prices in Hawaii. To a certain extent, that's true. The huge "off-price" retailers are shipping directly to their stores from the mainland instead of setting up island-based distribution centers. Warehousing on the mainland is so computer based high tech that they can monitor their inventory very closely and know exactly when to ship. They don't need to set up distribution centers here and keep large stock on hand. There is a pent-up demand in Hawaii for discount shopping. Hooray for Costco, Wal-Mart, and K-Mart. Hawaii welcomes you with open arms and open wallets!

Great Coffee!

Kona Coffee is a gourmet item. Kona is the only place in the United States where coffee is grown commercially and it is delicious. Grown on shaded mountain slopes above Kailua, these exceptionally rich tasting, pampered beans are blended by coffee merchants around the world to add flavor to otherwise bland varieties. In Kona, you can buy your coffee beans directly from the growers.

For a free tour of a coffee farm in Kona, phone **Old Hawaiian Coffee Farm** at 328-2277. Also, the Komo family owns a coffee farm and small store in Holualoa above the post office. You can buy their packaged, fresh ground coffee in the store. The aroma and essence of this coffee will make you want to go back for seconds!

Another pit stop could be the **Ferrari Coffee Plantation** in Holualoa. They're on Hwy-180 Holualoa. Phone 322-6713 for directions. Complimentary coffee is served, and if you buy 3 lb. you might be able to talk them into a 12 oz. bag freebie.

Coffee Retailers and Cafes

Bad Ass Coffee Co.	1-800-338-7139	or 322-2646
Holuakoa Cafe (Holualoa,Kona)		332-Cafe
Kohala Coffee Mill		889-5577
Waimea Coffee & Co.		885-4472

If you buy all of your food at retail prices from the supermarket your food expenses will cost $380 to $400 per month for two. But if you are willing to grow a few fruits, such as papayas and bananas, and/or buy your vegetables and fruits at the farmer's market, and use the other suggestions in this Chapter, you can slash your food bill for two adults to $300 per month.

Transportation; Gas and Oil

Roads on the Big Island are excellent, except for the Saddle Road which winds between the two mountains and is best avoided. Driving a car around the island is a relaxing pastime. One unbelievable view after another invites you to pause, park the car, and snap a picture. The trip around the island ordinarily takes about six hours, but if you stop to sample malasadas, to marvel over the views, and take a nap in the shade of a coconut tree, the trip can stretch into manana. Luckily roads are smooth, wide, and no potholes!

Hilo and Kona airports are roughly one hundred miles apart. Although the price of gas and oil is much higher than on the mainland, local residents put much less mileage on their cars. After all, your longest trip is around the island. A drive of one or two hours is a **big excursion!**

The price of gasoline, (regular, no-lead) in Hilo is currently $1.769 per gallon; $0.10 more in Kona. No satisfactory explanation has been given in spite of numerous complaints. Whatever the traffic will bear? (The State of Hawaii is currently suing the oil companies charging them with conspiracy to fix (high) prices. The suit is schedule to come to trial in 2001).

Oil is best purchased at the supermarket rather than a service station.

There is a Hele-on (Let's go!) bus service offering island wide bus service at very reasonable rates. As we go to press the fare is $5.25 one way Hilo-Kona or Kona-Hilo. Better check with them as to scheduled departure times. Phone 808.961.8744. You can catch the Bus in Hilo on Kamehameha Ave. at the downtown bus terminal, and in Kona in front of Waldenbooks at the Lanihau Shopping Center. This fare is a terrific bargain.

Taxis are plentiful but expensive - $2.25 per mile, plus $1.85 for each piece of luggage.

One of the great bonuses you have going for you here is that you're in the good old U.S.A. We follow the same driving rules and regs. Go for green, go faster for orange, and stop on red. Just take it easy and slow down, because the scenery is so spectacular you might miss something if you whiz along over 55 mph.

Clothing

This factor in living costs can compensate for higher expenditures elsewhere. All you really need in Hawaii is a bathing suit, jeans, a couple of cotton shirts or blouses, one or two light sweaters and a rain jacket, shorts, and that's it! You don't even really need a pair of shoes, unless for church or jogging, as the local favorite footwear is rubber thong slippers. Dress is extremely casual island-wide. Muumuus are classy for the ladies. Don't forget to pin a flower in your hair, and you're all set.

Utilities

Power bills in Hawaii, generally speaking, are low even though thermal unit costs are high, because the climate is so temperate and even that central air-conditioning and central heating are not incorporated into homes. Windows are usually louvred glass panes which are left open for ventilation. Ovens and washer/dryers are powered by either gas or electricity. A power bill for two people in a 1,200 foot dwelling on average could run between $35 to $75 per month. If window airconditioners are used occasionally, during the summer months at sea level, the power bill could be as much as $100.

Likewise, water bills are moderate. If you have city water and water your yard three times per week for an hour's time, your monthly bill averages $35 to $39 for **two** months. Rain takes care of the watering chores much of the time. (In Hilo, **all** the time!) And if you use catchment tanks, water is free - manna from heaven!

Telephone service is provided by GTE Hawaiian Telephone Co., and you have a choice of 3 long-distance carriers, A.T. & T., Sprint, and M.C.I. For local calls, basic service for a private line in Hilo and Kona runs about $40 per month. In outlying areas, $38 per month pays for a party line. A private line is charged at $55. Inter-island and mainland calls can quickly add more.

Cable TV service standard package is available in most areas and the cost is $30.73 per month plus .04 F.C.C. user fee, $1.88 franchise fee, and $1.80 general excise tax. Where there is no service offered, residents substitute satellite dishes. Overall, utilities are quite reasonable. Not having to heat your home is a real benefit. Many residents have been installing solar panels, using sunlight to heat water, for additional savings.

LIVING ON $1,000 PER MONTH

Since the biggest dent in your monthly budget comes from housing, you'd need to relocate where housing costs are low to keep within this budget. If you don't want to do yard work and prefer condo living, you'd look for a condo or apartment in Hilo or Waikoloa.

To rent a home, or to buy an existing house or lot on which to build, for the lowest price you'd look first in Ka'u, next in South Kona near the Ka'u border, then in Volcano/Puna. If you own your own home free and clear, or you rent, two adults can live on $1,000 per month in these areas. It's helpful if you have a small yard to grow a few fruit trees and veggies. In certain parts of Ka'u, the lava soil is crumbled black lava rock but it is so amazingly rich in nutrients that with the addition of water, fruit trees and veggies sprout like weeds.

There are about two thousand families living in the District of Ka'u in HOVE (Hawaiian Ocean View Estates subdivision). Living there is like living on a farm in a rural area. You do a little fishing and gardening. Although there is a small neighborhood shopping center, for lower prices you'd drive into town (**Kealekekua** or **Kailua**) once a week to stock up on groceries.

Unless you have a satellite dish, you read or rent videos for home entertainment instead of watching television. The climate is perfect and ocean views are exquisite. There is a gorgeous, practically deserted white sand beach at the shoreline.

Hove (Hawaiian Ocean View Estates)

Two can live very cheaply in this area:

MONTHLY BUDGET FOR TWO ADULTS

Rent	$500
Food	300
Electricity	35
Water*(catchment water)	0

```
Phone                              38
(Party line. $58 if private line)
Gas & Oil                          50
Misc. (haircuts, videos, etc.)    77
                              -------
Total                         $1,000
```

*Normally there is sufficient rainfall to supply all of your water needs. Perhaps once a year you might experience three to five days of dry weather. If it becomes necessary to buy water, phone Charley Young at 929-7384 or Mobile 936-0471. Charley's been in business there for twenty years and will deliver 5,000 gallons for $150. He also does land clearing, driveways, and house pads.

If you owned your own home free and clear by buying or building, there would be room in this budget for savings. Annual property taxes island wide are low, only .35% of a home's value. This means your property taxes on a $100,000 home would only be $350. This compares closely to Montgomery, Alabama, where property taxes are .30%. Taxes are certainly much less than in California for newcomers.

This budget could be duplicated in Volcano, Puna, Hilo, or Waikoloa if you don't care for a remote location.

Hawaii has excellent group medical and dental plans - the most advanced in the nation. Since the Prez has so far not been successful with his universal health coverage, then, if you're not already covered, you might want to open a small business or look for part-time employment (20 hours or more) in order to join a group plan .

To be sure, there's not room in this budget to hire a cleaning lady or gardener as in some Third World Countries, but the benefits of living in a virtually crime free environment under the protection of U.S. laws is priceless.

MEDICAL FACILITIES

The best medical facilities in the Hawaiian Islands are located in Honolulu. Honolulu's doctors are among the finest practicing physicians in the nation. Of the State's 80 hospitals, 67 are in Honolulu. Queen's, Straub, Kuakini, Kaiser, St. Francis, Children's, Pali Momi, Kapiolani, Pali Momi - all have excellent reputations. Of the States's over 5,000 licensed physicians, approximately 220 are on the Big Island.

This concentration of doctors in Honolulu creates a situation wherein most of the specialists are there. If you need to see a specialist, then, more likely than not, you would catch a half-hour flight to Honolulu, and board the Bus at Honolulu airport (fare $.85) to your doctor's office. Several M.D. specialists live on Oahu, but visit the Big Island once or twice a month to see patients. Appointments need to be made 30 - 60 days in advance.

In a life-threatening emergency, your local doctor might Med-Evac you to Honolulu on the local inter-island air ambulance. For everyday minor ailments - cuts, bruises, hayfever, skin rashes, flu, etc. - you can certainly get adequate care on the Big Island. Physician office visits cost approximately $40.00 to $80.00.

Hawaii County (the entire island) has a total of about 738 hospital beds. Of these, 252 are acute-care and 486 long-term or nursing home beds. There is a shortage of long-term care beds on all of the islands, partly because the State did not anticipate the change in the customs of elder care among the population soon enough to build additional facilities. For many years families took care of elderly parents at home. Even today, families put their elders in nursing homes with great reluctance. However, today most wives work, which makes caring for aged parents at home very difficult.

On the Big Island, there are hospitals in Hilo, Honokaa, Kohala, Waimea, and Kona. Five years ago Kona Hospital added a kidney dialysis unit, which has been much appreciated by patients who no longer have to go to Honolulu for dialysis. There are nursing homes in Hilo, Pahala, and Kona. West Hawaii is ecstatic over the completion of a state-of-the art private hospital (North Kona Community Hospital), which opened in Kamuela in 1996 and which has attracted an excellent staff.

Dental care on Hawaii is excellent. There are about 82 dentists on the island, more than enough to service the population. Until recently, for a root canal or difficult extraction, you would have gone to see a specialist dental surgeon in Honolulu. Now, however, there are excellent oral surgeons on the island.

BUSINESS OPPORTUNITIES

It's been said many times that to succeed in business in Hawaii you need not only know-how, but know-who, and have deep pockets. But Horatio Alger stories have happened here just as well as anywhere in the U.S. Some people have the knack of looking around and seeing a need or vacuum, and filling it. Others look around and either don't see the need, or don't have the energy, know-how, or persistence to fill it. For those with an entrepreneurial bent, Hawaii offers many opportunities, for it typically lags behind the mainland in trends and technology. For example there is a much heralded 21 million dollar fiber-optics cable being laid now between the Big Island and Maui, the last link in a statewide fiber-optic chain. This will help the business community grow, meaning additional jobs and a growing economy for the island. But this is already old technology on the mainland.

Hawaii has lagged about 10 years behind the trend toward mass retailing seen on the mainland. The warehouse retailers and discount centers have recently discovered that (1) Hawaii's household buying power is about 25% higher than the national average (all those working wives), Hawaii is ranked 3rd in the U.S. at $31,000 per household in terms of retail sales (we love to buy!), Hawaii has very little retail space per capita compared to California or Florida, (4) Hawaii residents are extremely frugal and value conscious consumers who clip coupons like mad.

New, diversified agriculture is badly needed on Hawaii, because of sugar's decline. The Big Island does offer relatively inexpensive rent and low-cost land compared to Oahu, and the new cable will allow residents to live here and conduct business anywhere in the world.

Let's look at some of the needs and potential commercial possibilities in Ka'u, reprinted by kind permission of Roger Bason, Institute for a Sustainable Future, Pahala, Hawaii 96777, as published in the July 1994 edition of the Ka'u Landing Newspaper:

Forests

Since the sugar industry is phasing out in that area, much reforestation is needed to replace 5,000 acres of existing sugar cane and private land reforestation with native species of wood, mixed hardwood, bamboo (for production of rattan furniture).

Ka'u residents need nursery development of 2.4 million trees (an average of 400 trees per acre with a 20% replant factor), which would produce jobs for nursery employment, replanting, maintenance and harvesting, transport and local processing centers.

They would like to see more nature trails and jobs for trail development, maintenance, hunting guides, and ecotourism in the renewable forests.

They would also like to see more production of herbs, fruit, flowers, beekeeping and honey.

Medicine

As the population grows, the area could certainly use a medical and dental clinic.

There is potential for growing and marketing medicinal herbs.

Commercial

There are terrific locations for a children's summer camp with horseback riding, archery, and other outdoor activities.

A potential location for an adult Outward Bound retreat, with survival lessons given.

Good locations for an adult health and beauty spa.

Food

The residents would like to see the value of all food products produced in the area increased by 30%. More macadamia nut trees and fruit trees need to be planted. Establish a Farmer's Market as in Hilo and Kona. Establish spice plantations. Expand dairy production. Nobody is making butter or cheese on the island except for goat and feta cheese.

Set definable and measurable goals for aquaculture, fishing, and seaweed production.

Fuel

There is a need for increased solar installations, perhaps as many as 500 to 1,000 applications in homes, parks, swimming pools, and light industry.

There is a need to develop energy production from a variety of sources including renewable fuels such as burning paper waste, green waste, ethanol and wood for fuel mix, all locally generated or locally grown.

There is a need to install extensive energy conservation measures to reduce energy waste.

Perhaps a rural electrical co-operative could be organized.

Replace propane uses with methane gas production from home scale or community scale units. Construct a Biogas unit in Pahala or Naalehu and 500 small scale units in order to convert from propane to methane use by the year 2000.

Education

Academies need to be set up to teach trade skills and higher learning. They need to teach construction and marine skills.

Cultural and Recreation Development

The Sea Mountain Golf Course and resort in Punaluu has recently been purchased by the Robert's Tour and Travel Co.

Local residents would have liked to see the resort purchased by the community and used as a community resource.

Spaceport

The State of Hawaii is no longer still considering Palima Point in Kau as a rocket launching facility. There has been much environmental opposition which was weighed against new job opportunities, improved communications, adequate and reliable electric power, better schools, homes, improved medical services and usual development spin-off service industries. (McDonalds, Sears, Penney's, auto dealerships etc.) If this comes to pass in another five or ten years, the face of Ka'u will change forever, and if you would want to open a pancake house or franchise, the increase in population will support your dream. For now, it is a beautiful, rural area with great potential.

Hamakua

The same situation exists on the Hamakua Coast since Hamakua Sugar Co.has phased out operations. Much rich soil land is available and the same opportunities exist there as in Kau. Hamakua is especially well-suited for growing macadamia nuts, and for growing flowers. They need little cultivation. Rainfall is ample. Stands of wild ginger grow by the roadside. The area is wild, beautiful, and sparsely populated at present.

Whatever products or services you would supply would need to be marketed in Hilo or Kona, shipped by air, or by inter-island barge (Young Bros.) at Kawaihae Harbor, or Matson in Hilo.

It seems as if the economic future of Hamakua, and indeed all of the Big Island will greatly depend on diversified agriculture to replace the sugar plantations.

Hilo

Hilo is fairly well developed with a light industrial base and you can obtain most goods and services there, although, if you buy all of your foodstuffs in the supermarkets, it has been estimated that your breadbasket cost will be 35% higher than on the mainland. So there is much room for improved products to sell for a lesser price. There are few discount houses in Hilo - Cost-U-Less and a new Wal Mart. Trader Joe, where are you? This alone should ring an entrepreneurial bell.

Your best bet in Hilo is to concentrate on a service business. I know of an entrepreneur in Kona who started up an appliance repair business. He offers a yearly contract to service home appliances for a yearly fee. Business, he says, is booming. No one is doing this in the Hilo area.

Hilo is ripe for a sophisticated health spa offering aerobic classes, swimming, and exercise equipment in an attractive facility.

Just look around in communities on the mainland and see what isn't being offered in Hilo. For example, there are no leather shops offering cowboy boots and leather coats such as those found in El Paso, Texas. There's not much in the way of import shops. A really great hamburger hamlet would be popular among the locals - a Wendy's or Denny's, or Bob's Big Boy. Local residents have much more disposable income than many areas on the mainland. They'll buy if they like the product. The discount houses found that out in Honolulu. Costco's Honolulu store is said to be their most profitable in the nation. Now they've moved into West Hawaii. Inevitably, as the population grows, East Hawaii will grow also, and offer additional business opportunties.

West Hawaii

New Retailing

Costco's store in Honolulu quickly became the top moneymaker in the Costco chain. Costco just recently opened in Kona, bringing new jobs to the community.

The large discount stores such as Costco with its competitive pricing has helped to make living on Hawaii more affordable for all. Big Island residents are extremely appreciative of Costco's entrance into the community.

Tourism

Tourism has been the driving force behind Hawaii's economy, and tourists naturally gravitate toward sunny West Hawaii's shores, Hotel construction has temporarily outstripped demand and the competition from new, less expensive Asian resorts in Bali, Thailand, Kuala Lumpur, and Vietnam is intensifying. Hawaii has been caught between recessions in Japan and California, but tourism is finally on the upswing again.

Tourism is the magnet that draws economic opportunities for new bed and breakfasts, rental cars, land, sea, and air adventure tours etc. The new buzz word now in tourism is "ecotourism." Visitors vacation here to experience Hawaii's distinct personality and diversity. They enjoy the great climate, lively hotels, terrific beaches and our special ecological attractions: rain forests, volcanoes, perfumed flowers, tropical birds, and indigenous wildlife.

The best nature preserves are hidden away from civilization in rain forests and isolated beach coves. The ecotourists are not looking for another Waikiki. They are looking for peaceful, natural surroundings away from the plastic, concrete urban life. Here Hawaii excels. To capitalize on this trend, entrepreneurs are needed to provide tourist accommodations and services and help to preserve the natural environment by promoting environmental understanding and education. Ecotourism is the wave of the future for tourism in West Hawaii. Note: the first tour agency offering "eco-tours" has just opened in Kona.

Owning a Business

It seems that newcomers who have opened a business here and run it successfully are those who look around the community, see what is lacking and try to fill the void. In other words, those who fall in love with the place and try to find a way to stay here, rather than those whose primary objective is to make money. That secret to success has worked elsewhere and it works here.

One local businessman, a malihini (newcomer) from Iran, saw that there was no restaurant here serving Japanese food. Although he didn't know beans about cooking Japanese food, he decided to give it a try. Ah, so! His little restaurant became so popular he's now open seven days a week to keep up with demand. Certainly there are other success stories and room for other energetic entrepreneurs in West Hawaii.

RECREATIONAL AND CULTURAL FACILITIES

Points of Interest

Volcanoes National Park

One of the most interesting and diverse parks in the country. Admission $5.00. Don't miss Halemaumau Crater, the Thurston Lava Tube, the Chain of Craters road, sulphur banks, and of course, the main attraction, lava entering the sea.

Hilo Town

Check in at the Lyman Museum for a map of downtown Hilo. Cost $1.00. Hilo is great for a walking tour on a sunny day. Don't miss Rainbow Falls next to the Hilo Memorial Hospital in Piihonua. Also take in the beautiful Liliuokalani Gardens on Banyan Drive.

Akaka Falls

Not to be missed. This cascading waterfall boasts a 400 foot drop, set in an exquisite natural tropical forest of tree ferns and exotic flowers. Honomu, Hamakua Coast

Waipio Valley

Breathtaking view overlooking a 900 foot drop into the valley with its black sand beach and gigantic waterfalls.

63

Parker Ranch

Set in Waimea, the ranch covers 225,000 acres. Visit the ranch center in Kamuela town, and its little museum.

Pololu Valley Lookout

Awesome views in Kohala. Look for the island of Maui. Hwy. 270 in North Kohala.

Puuhonua O Honaunau

A national park in South Kona. Admission $2.00. This is the former Hawaiian City of Refuge, a sacred place where Hawaiians who had broken the ancient "kapus" (actions which were forbidden), could seek safety and refuge from the king's wrath within the confines of the city. Site of religious carvings or totems.

South Point U.S.A.

The southernmost point in the United States, possible landing of the first native settlers from the Marquesas Islands. Look for the green sand beach nearby.

Heiaus and Petroglyphs

Look for the ancient religious temples (heiaus) on the Kohala Coast. Petroglyphs (stick carvings in lava rock) may be seen at the Royal Waikoloan Resort Hotel and in many other areas in Kohala.

Restaurants

Fine Dining

In this chapter we intentionally have not included restaurants located in the major hotels. All of the major hotels offer fine dining and serve meals fit (and eaten by) kings and presidents. The major hotels serve lavish buffet brunches on Sundays and Holidays. The Mauna Kea Beach Hotel is famous worldwide for its incomparable Sunday brunch. Also offering excellent brunches are the Mauna Lani, the King Kam, Kona Hilton, Kona Surf, and the Naniloa in Hilo. Each of the major hotels also provide sumptuous lunches and dinners, but they are pricey. We recommend the hotel dining rooms and these other restaurants for fine dining:

Jameson's By the Sea

Jameson's is noted for its seafood and combination platters. Oceanfront on Alii Drive next to Magic White Sand Beach. Phone 329-3195. Prices range from $10 to $30.

Fisherman's Landing

The Landing is noted for its wonderful steak and seafood dishes. Oceanfront on Alii Drive next to the Kona Inn Shopping Village Phone 326-2555. Prices range from $15 to $40.

La Bourgogne

Fantastic French cooking. Kuakini Plaza South Hwy 11. Phone 329-6711. Prices range from $15 to $30. Lunch is not served.

Merriman's

Located in Kamuela. Chef Merriman has a heavyweight reputation. He uses only the freshest fruits and vegetables. Outstanding food and service. Opelo Plaza. Phone 885-6822. Prices range from $30 to $40.

Roussels

Located in Hilo. New Orleans style Cajun cooking. 60 Keawe St. Phone 935-5111. Prices range from $10 to $30.

Moderate Dining

Quinn's

A small bar/restaurant oozing South Seas charm. Lunch and dinner. On Palani Road near the Kona Beach Hotel and almost opposite the Chevron station. Fantastic fresh fish sandwiches. Price range $8 to $15. Phone 329-3822.

Kona Ranch House

Terrific old Hawaii atmosphere. Coffee shop plus a separate dining room. Food is excellent. Sits on a hill in town on Kuakini Hwy a half-block south of the lower traffic light and next to the Shell service station. Phone 329-7061.
Prices range from $10 to $15.

Wakefield Gardens

Well-known for its famous tuna salad in papaya boat. Homemade sandwiches, soups, vegetarian fare, Kona coffee, and fresh baked pies. Located in Honaunau, Kona. Call for directions. Phone 328-9930.
Price Range $10 to $15.

Bree's Garden

Just behind the Texaco station on Hwy 19 in Kamuela. Their food is fabulous. Prices range from $7.00 to $15.00 for lunch, more for dinner. Phone 885-8849

Edelweiss

Mamalahoa Hwy as you enter Kamuela driving toward Hilo. Across from Opelo Plaza. Excellent German dishes, fresh fish, venison, beef, veal, and excellent roast duck. Phone 885-6800. Prices range from $10 to $40.

KK Tei Restaurant

In Hilo. Excellent Japanese as well as American food. Noted for its friendly service as well. 1550 Kamehameha Ave. Phone 961-3791.
Prices range from $10 to $30.

Denny's

Crossroads Shopping Center near Safeway and above Wal-Mart in Kona. Open 24 hours. Great breakfast menu. $6.00 to $15.00. Phone 334.1313.

Harrington's

In Hilo. Tremendous variety menu with an emphasis on seafood. Reed's Bay. 135 Kalanianiole Hwy. Phone for directions. Phone 961-4966.
Price range $10 to $30.

Volcano House

Awesome setting overlooking Halemaumau Crater. Steak and seafood. Exceptional desserts. Hawaii Volcanoes National Park Phone 967-7321. Price range $10 to $30.

Edward's At The Terrace

Located oceanfront in the Kanaloa at Kona condominium complex by the swimming pool. (Just below the Keauhou

Shopping Center). Features Mediterranean cuisine. Serves breakfast, lunch, and dinner. Phone 322-1434.

Price range $10 to $30.

Inexpensive Dining

Huggo's.

Great hamburgers, fresh fish, and prime rib.
Alii Drive Kailua, just before the Kona Hilton Hotel. Oceanfront. Phone 329-1493. Price range $10 to $15.

Ocean View Inn

Alii Drive Just across the street from the seawall in downtown Kailua a half-block from the King Kam Hotel. Very popular with a wide menu variety. Excellent Chinese food and local dishes. Phone 329-9998. Price range $10 to $15.

Jolly Roger

On the ocean. Good seafood, salads, and mahimahi. Next door to Hale Halawai Park on Alii Drive in downtown Kailua. At 9:30 PM a live band livens up the night. Phone 329-1344. Prices range from $10 to $30.

Manago Hotel Restaurant

Long a local favorite and noted for their bountiful breakfasts. Emphasis on family cooking. Succulent pork chops. Breakfast, lunch, and dinner. Captain Cook on Hwy 11. Phone 323-2642 Price range $10 to $15.

Dick's Coffee House

In Hilo. Located in the Prince Kuhio Plaza. Emphasis on family cooking, meat loaf, pork chops, and an extensive menu.

Prices are incredibly low.   Phone 959-4401.   Prices less than $10.

Sam Choy's Diner

Located in the new Industrial Area, in Kona.   73-5576 Kauhola St., Bay 1. . Excellent breakfast and plate lunches. For teriyaki, as the locals say - it's onolicious!   Phone 326.1545. $10-$15.

Additional Suggestions:

Volcano Country Club

Hawaii Volcanoes National Park at the 30 Mile Marker, across from Kilauea Military Camp. Phone 967-7721.

The Aloha Cafe

In Kainaliu, about halfway between Kailua and Captain Cook. Phone 322-3383 for directions.

Cafe Pesto

Kawaihae Center, Kohala Coast. Phone 882-1071
You won't go hungry on the island, that's for sure. McDonald's, Wendy's, and a good number of mainland fast food eateries are here, too, along with super pizza parlors. (Try Biannelli's in the Pines Plaza - Kona, 75-240 Nani Kailua Dr., Phone 326-4800. They deliver also).

Bakery goods, Ice cream and Candy

Bakery goods

Mamane Street Bakery - located in downtown Honokaa on the Hamakua Coast.   Wholesale and retail.   For quiches,

69

foccasias, croissants, desserts, pastries, cookies, espresso and cappucino. Phone 775-9478

Robert's Bakery in Hilo - two locations in Hilo. Noted for its pies, croissants, and doughnuts. Downtown Phone 935-0824 Waiakea Phone 935-2230

Holy's Bakery in Kapaau, Kohala is famous throughout the islands for its apple and peach pies, and cookies. You can buy them frozen in supermarkets throughout the islands. Phone 889-6865.

Chris Bakery in Kealekekua, Kona on Hwy 11. Noted for malasadas (Portuguese doughnuts) and sweet rolls or fruit filled pastries. Phone 323-2444.

Ice cream

Tropical Dreams ice cream factory and cafe in Kapaau, Kohala makes the best home-made ice cream and sorbets you've ever tasted. They are open daily from Mon. through Sat. from 11 to 5 and on Sun. from 1 - 5. You can purchase their products around the island at the following outlets:

> **Waipio Art Works** - Waipio
> **Hawaii Mac Nut Plantation** - Honokaa
> **Tropical Dreams** - Kawaihae
> **Sugar and Spice** - in the Parker Ranch Shopping Center
> **El Gecko** - Waikoloa
> **Island Lava Java** - downtown Kailua
> **Kealekekua Antiques and Art** - Kealekekua, Kona

Baskin-Robbins operates outlets around the island in the Keauhou Shopping Center (Kona), in Hilo, Keaau, and in Waimea.

Candies

Kailua Candy Co.- Kona - has moved a half block away from its old location. They are still in the Old Industrial area, but now are located across from West Hawaii Today. Open 7 days a week from 7 am to 6 pm. Phone 329-2522.

Big Island Candy Co. - Hilo - 500 Kalanianiole Hwy. offers free candy-making tours. Phone 935-8890.

You can also sample candies at the macadamia nut visitor centers around the island.

Hawaii Macadamia Nut Plantation
Phone 775-7201

Lodging -Best Bed and Breakfasts

These are becoming increasingly popular as an alternative to staying at hotels:

Holualoa Inn, Kona   324-1121
         Box 222, Holualoa, Kona 96725

B & B Hawaiian Islands	1-800-258-7895
Bed & Breakfast Hawaii	1-800-733-1622
Bed & Breakfast Statewide	1-800-288-4666
Carson's Volcano Cottage	1-800-845-LAVA
	(808)967-7683
Chalet Kilauea.	(808)967-7786
Hale Kai	(808)935-6330
Hale Maluhia	(808)329-5773
Waipio Wayside	1-800-833-8849
Wild Ginger Inn	(808)935-5556

Note: Prices range from a low of $39 per night at Wild Ginger, double accommodation, through medium $65 per night at the Volcano, to $100 per night in Kona.

Best Beaches

The island has some of the best beaches in the world. Some of them are off the main road and you'll have to ask directions to get there. All of the hotel beaches have public access and are open to the public (it's the law.) The State of Hawaii retains title to all of the beaches, and if you can get there without crossing private property, it's yours to use.

Kona

Magic Sands, also called White Sands

Right in Kailua. Terrific body surfing. Waves are high in winter. Wave action continually removes then redeposits the sand. Very popular beach.

Kahaluu Beach Park

Right in Kailua. Noted for terrific snorkeling. Swim with the turtles and feed the fish frozen peas.

Kamakahonu Lagoon

Right in Kailua. Fronts the Hotel King Kam. Place to go if you like calm water. Great for children.

Old Kona Airport Beach

120 acre site with tide pool inlets and a small white sand beach, great for children.

Makalawena Beach

If you're looking for a beautiful deserted white sand beach with great swimming, just walk north along the shoreline from

Old Kona Airport Beach and you'll stumble on to Makalawena Beach. A beach for lovers or would be lovers.

Kaunaoa Beach

Undoubtedly one of the most beautiful beaches in the entire world. Fronts the Mauna Kea Hotel. Parking spaces are reserved for the public at the southern end of the hotel lot. Access is through a path from the service road to the beach. This beach is reef protected. Swimming is superlative. (Sorry, can't help raving.)

Hapuna Beach

Huge white sand beach. Very popular because it's so sunny. But watch out for rip tides in the winter. Don't ever go swimming at this beach alone and don't go too far out. Great for whale watching in the winter.

Kiholo Bay

Black sand beach. There's a large, spring-fed pool created by a lava flow. A natural swimming pool.

Kalahuipuaa

Fronts the Mauna Lani Bay Hotel. It's a jewel. Small and calm.

Anaehoomalu Bay

Don't miss this one. It's one of the best beaches on the island. Huge beach. Great for swimming, snorkeling, and windsurfing. Fronts the Royal Waikoloan Hotel, just renamed the Outrigger Waikoloa Beach Hotel..

Samuel Spencer Beach Park

At Kawaihae Bay. Calm waters, great for snorkeling and swimming. Lots of marine life. Good for children.

South Kona

You can skip Hookena Beach Park and Milolii Beach Park, neither is very inviting.

Ka'u

Punaluu Beach Park

Black sand beach. Part of it has green sand (crushed olivine) Be careful. Powerful rip tide, but there's a nice protected inlet at the north end which is best for safe swimming. Nice place to picnic. Very picturesque.

Forget Puna. The Kaimu Black Sand Beach there that was a terrific swimming beach has been covered over with lava.

Hilo

Onekahakaha Beach Park

Nice park. Good swimming and lifeguards.

James Kealoha Park

It's okay. Nice swimming lagoon but no sand beach. Good for picnicking.

Coconut Island

Very picturesque island in Hilo Bay reached by a bridge. Good for picnicking. There's an old 20 foot diving tower. Careful. Rocky shoreline.

Kolekole Beach Park

There's a natural pool fed by a waterfall. Great swimming. Very picturesque site but not so easy to find. You'll have to ask for directions as it's tucked away under a bridge.

You can also swim on top of Rainbow and Akaka Falls. The water is cold. Youngsters still do so, but you have to be agile to get there. Don't try it unless you're a superior athlete.

North Kohala

This area has two beaches, **Waipio Bay** and **Keokea Beach Park**. I wouldn't recommend swimming here. It's too dangerous. There's heavy surf and unexpected rip tides.

Golf

The island has superlative golf courses, most with fantastic ocean views, some with the Pacific Ocean as a water hazard:

Volcano Golf and Country Club,18 holes	967-7222
Hilo Municipal Course, 18 holes	959-7711
Naniloa Country Club - Hilo,9 holes	935-3000
Hamakua Country Club, Honokaa,9 holes	775-7244
Hapuna Golf Course 18 holes	880-3000
Waikoloa Village Golf Course, 18 holes 883-9621	
Waikoloa Beach Golf Club , 18 holes	885-6060
Mauna Lani Golf Course, 18 holes	885-6655
Mauna Kea Beach Hotel, 18 holes	882-7222
(Called Hawaii's finest by Golf Digest)	
Kona Country Club,27 holes	322-2595
Makalei Country Club, 18 holes 325-6625	
Discovery Harbor Golf Course, 18 holes	322-2595
Sea Mountain, Punaluu,18 holes	928-6222

There is also a Municipal Course under consideration in Kona, but it won't be open for play until the cows come home.

Tennis

The hotel courts are reserved for hotel guests, but there are at least 20 county parks around the island that have courts open to the public. Phone the Department of Parks and Recreation in Hilo at 961-8311 and they will tell you where the courts are in your area.

Charter Fishing

A "clean sweep" in local fishing circles means that you've caught one of each of Hawaii's four outstanding gamefish: ahi (tuna), mahimahi (dolphin fish - not the mammal), marlin, and ono (bonefish). If you do boat all four, you get to fly the broom when you reenter the harbor. Here to help you acquire legitimate bragging rights for sportfishing are:

Summer Rain Sportfishing	**325-7558**
High Flier Sportfishing	**325-6374**
Janet "B"	**325-6374**
Omega	**325-7593**
Mariah Sportfishing	**326-4181**

There are activities desks at the hotels and in the shopping centers that can also make reservations for you for various activities.

Art Galleries

There are some beautiful galleries in the mega-resort hotels but they are pricey. Here's a list of local galleries with interesting paintings and artifacts at more modest prices.

Upcountry Connection	**885-0623**
Waimea Center, Kamuela	

Cook's Discoveries   **855-3633**
Waimea Center Kamuela

Volcano Art Center   **967-8222**
Hawaii Volcanoes National Park

Cottage Gallery   **328-9392**
South Kona, Hwy. 11 between mile
markers 106-105

Ackerman Galleries   **889-5971**
Kapaau town, Hwy 270 North

Wo On Gallery   **889-5002**
Kohala, .7 mile past mile marker 25
Hwy 270 North

Horseback Riding

Naalapa Trail Rides.   **775-0330**
Horses are gentle. Wranglers who guide you are experienced and knowledgeable. Their Waipio Valley ride takes you through some of the most beautiful valleys and trails. A second trail ride will take you through the Kohala Mountains to Kahua Ranch. Wildlife seen include wild pigs, turkeys, pheasant, quail, and owls. Book ahead as these rides are popular.

Fallbrook Trail Rides   **322-1818**
Ride on a grassy bridle path through Kona's tropical rain forest.

Dahana Ranch   **885-0057**
Open-range ride in the uplands of Waimea

By Land Sea, and Air

Nautilus Submarines   **326-2003**
Atlantis Submarines   **329-6626**

Captain Zodiac	329-3199
Body Glove Snorkeling Cruise	326-7122
Fair Wind (to Kealekekua Bay)	322-2788
Captain Beans Dinner Cruises	329-2955
Lanakila Trimaran Cruise	987-3999
Chris Bike Adventures	326-4600
Papillon Helicopters	329-0551
Blue Hawaiian Helicopters	961-5600
UFO Parasail.	325-5UFO
Sea Paradise Scuba.	322-2500
Kona Kayak	326-2922

Theatres

Kona Marketplace Cinema	329-4488
World Square Theatre, Kona	329-4070
Hualalai Theatres, Kona	329-6641
Prince Kuhio Theatres, Hilo	959-4595
Waiakea Theatres, Hilo	935-9747
Aloha Performing Arts, Kona	322-9924
Kilauea Theatre, Volcano	967-8222

Getting Here

If you decided to fly in and take a look at the island, you would need to rent or buy a car here, or ship your car over. Public transportation just won't cut it. It's an easy task to ship your car.

There are three cargo companies that service Hawaii. Sea Land, Aloha Cargo, and Matson Navigation Co. Matson is the oldest and most experienced. It ships from Long Beach, San Francisco, Seattle, or Portland. All you have to do is drive it, for example, to Matson Navigation at Terminal Island, Long Beach, California. They'll take care of it for you. It costs around $850.00 depending on size and weight. It takes about three weeks to arrive in Hilo. Then you'd want to stay in a hotel or one of the popular bed and breakfasts for a couple of days.

You could then make arrangements to rent a house or condo for a few months until you get your "feet on the ground." Then, on your own or with a realtor's help, you could find something more permanent. Incidentally, shipping furniture is not cost effective. You can buy furniture here. Of course you'd want to bring articles of sentimental value, if any. But shipping a car is practical, as cars sell for more here than on the mainland.

Of course you can ship your furniture in a 24 foot container ($2,200 or $2,400 to ship, depending on departure port). Matson can supply you with a 40 foot container if you have tons of stuff to ship. You can also rent a partial container, but it's not a good idea to mix your things in with other people's household goods.

Now, you already know more about the Big Island than 99% of the newcomers (malihini) that visit. Your best bet in making arrangements to get here is to watch for specials offered by Hawaiian Airlines, American, Continental, Delta, TWA, Northwest, and United Airlines. Instead of flying directly to Hilo or Kona, you might want to spend a few days on Oahu. You could then fly inter-island on Hawaiian Airlines, the local inter-island carrier with the perfect safety record.

Getting here is easy and surprisingly inexpensive. Compare airline prices with what a travel agent can do for you. One of the big attractions Hawaii has to offer is that it has the flavor of a foreign country, yet offers a safe comfort zone of American familiarity (English is spoken, no money changing problems, it has your favorite hamburger hamlets and TV programs.)

The adventure of a lifetime is waiting for you on the Big Island, and when you see it all, you just might decide to spend the rest of your life here. You could just get used to that!

CHAPTER 3. MAUI, THE VALLEY ISLE

Maui is a hop, skip, and a jump from Honolulu with a flight time of only a half-hour to Kahului Airport. This second youngest of the Hawaiian Islands has a total land area of only 729 square miles. Maui is small, measuring only 48 miles long and 26 miles across at its widest point, yet for many visitors it remains the ultimate island experience. From jet blue ink-stained waters off Lahaina where humpback whales cavort each winter, to the misty slopes of Haleakala Volcano, Maui's beauty is incandescent. I think of her as the radiant island.

CRIME FREE?

Maui has experienced such a dramatic spurt in population growth, that local residents say they no longer feel comfortable leaving doors unlocked. Burglaries are becoming a concern, along with an influx of pot-smoking mainlanders. Life is not quite so tranquil except perhaps in the remote Hana area or in upcountry Kula, Makawao, and Pukalani.

THE WEATHER

The weather is similar to that of the other Hawaiian Islands. Haiku in upcountry Maui rivals Hilo's rainfall. The beach areas of Kihei, Kaanapali, and Lahaina are dry and almost too hot in the summer. Upcountry Maui's temperature lends itself to cooler, more comfortable living year-round.

COST OF LIVING AND JOB SITUATION

Dismal. Because the island is so beautiful and so desirable, many would like to become residents. Jobs are few and far between, mostly associated with tourism, and wages are low. Again, if you have professional expertise, marketable skills, and local references, you might be able to find work. However, the outlook is not encouraging because the cost of living is so high.

Real estate sales and rental prices are much higher than on the Big Island. In Central Maui, in Wailuku or Kahului, you would pay $325,000 for a thirty year old frame house that you could purchase in the Mid-West for $55,000. (But there it wouldn't have the beautiful ocean view and perfect weather.) However, it isn't just the high-priced real estate. Food prices are also much higher than on the Big Island. **Everything is higher.** Maui has one K-mart store in Kahului, and a new Costco.

WHAT'S IT LIKE?

UPCOUNTRY (Kula, Makawao, Pukalani)

Let's climb up Highway 37 to dormant Haleakala Volcano ten thousand feet above sea level. We'll wind our way upland past incredible vistas of pineapple and sugar cane, green ranchlands and truck farms, fields of protea and carnations, and misty rain forests The volcano's northern slopes support the fertile green farmland of **Makawao** and **Kula,** and the small golf course community of **Pukalani.** Similar in many ways to the Big Island's Waimea District, this is smaller-sized ranch country, studded with sweet-smelling eucalyptus groves and upland forests of sandalwood, acacia (koa), candlenut (kukui), and ohia trees. Living in upcountry Maui is about as close to Paradise as you can get here on earth.

HANA

Haleakala's eastern coastline supports remote, tropical **Hana**, accessible only by small plane, or by a winding fifty-one mile drive from Kahului, replete with hair-pin turns and blind curves. If you ever needed a loud car horn, now's the time and this is the place. The scenery is spectacular and wild. Hana is still old Hawaii at its best. It became the favorite spot and the final resting place of Charles Lindbergh, near the Seven Sacred Pools of Ohe'o Gulch.

In Hana there is not much in the way of housing. You might be able to find a small cottage to rent for $700 per month, but

82

winter mudslides and torrential rains make the roads frequently impassable. Living here year round takes a four wheel drive and an adventurous spirit.

THE LAHAINA COAST (Kaanapali, Lahaina, Napili, Kapalua)

The Lahaina Coast is hot and dry. You inhale the pungent smell of seaweed drying in the sun. Small sailboats and larger schooners bob in the harbor. The water looks as if someone just spilled many bottles of dark blue ink over its surface. This area offers premiere swimming, surfing, snorkeling, scuba diving. Then there's fishing, sailing, para-sailing. Plus canoeing, tennis, and great golf. The beaches are superb. But everything - from food to rentals - is expensive. A small one-bedroom furnished apartment (not oceanfront) would be available on a long term lease for $900 to $1000 per month. Sales prices for many villas in Kaanapali and Kapalua are in the million dollar range.

CENTRAL MAUI - (Kahului, Wailuku)

This is not considered a tourist area, so rentals are lower here. It's pretty and green and about a half hour drive to the beaches. You could find a long term two bedroom apartment rental for $800 per month. The local supermarkets are not as pricey as in the beach areas.

KIHEI/WAILEA/MAKENA

This area is ringed with the soft white sand beaches for which Maui is world famous. Ocean colors range from a light turquoise edging the beach to deep, jet blue ink offshore. Hibiscus, bougainvillea, and coconut palms sway in the breeze. It's hard to feel stressed when you're lying on a beach under a blue sky and warm sun, with puffy white clouds drifting by. Thirty or forty years ago this area was affordable. Unfortunately, today its world class resorts and condominiums command world class prices.

LIVING IN MAUI ON $1,000 PER MONTH

Could two adults live on Maui on $1,000 per month? No way. There are a few, only a handful of small, older cottages available to rent upcountry on a long term basis for $650 to $850 per month. The vast majority of rentals island wide are quite high, and other living costs are stratospheric. For local information on rentals, subscribe to:

The Maui News
P. O. Box 550
Wailuku, Hi. 96793-0550
Phone: Local 242-6333 From Honolulu: 521-4653
From the mainland: 1-800-827-0347

There is not the abundant supply of low cost housing available as on the Big Island. If you choose Maui, a couple would need a minimum of $2000 per month to make ends meet, and that doesn't include regular restaurant dining.

Note that Maui County includes the islands of **Molokai** and **Lanai,** which seem to float offshore on the horizon. Molokai does not, at present, have a sufficient water supply to sustain much development, but it's worth a visit to see its beautiful East coast.

Lanai, the pineapple island, has two very upscale resort hotels, and some intriguing ship wrecks and petroglyphs, a golf course, fields of Dole pineapples, and not much else-which is in inself an attraction. You can still sleep out on the beach at night under a starry sky without worrying about intruders.

Maui is so very expensive, i.e. to rent or to buy real estate, that I'll limit additional information to moderate cost hotels, restaurants, and a description of Maui's best beaches. I doubt that very many of my readers can afford to shell out $350,000 and up for a house. You can find high density condominium complexes in (noisy) Kihei, and some small condos in Wailuku that are affordable, but quite small for the asking prices. ($100,000 to $200,000).

MODERATE HOTELS

MAUI BEACH HOTEL
Tel. 808.877-0051
Overlooks the harbor on Kaahumanu St. (Rt. 32) right next to Hoaloha Park. Not far from the airport and close to Maui Mall. Rates are $93.00 to $115.00, standard to oceanfront. More for suites..

MAUI PALMS HOTEL
Tel. 808.877-0051
Right next door to the Maui Beach. Less expensive. $60 - $80 for a standard to deluxe room.

MAUI SEASIDE
Tel. 808.877-3311
A stone's throw east of the above hotels. $80 to $140.

BANANA BUNGALOW
310 N. Market St.
Wailuku, Hi. 96793
808/244-5090 fax 808.846-3678
For backpackers and surfers. $29 single, $35 double and bunkbeds are less.

Maui has dozens of resorts, most of them pricey.
I've given you just a bare bones list above.
If you want a more detailed list of accommodations and restaurants, I suggest Frommer's Travel Guide 2000 Maui which includes a useful map.

MODERATE DINING

RAINBOW ROOM
808.877-0051
At the Maui Beach Hotel. Serves delicious buffet meals for breakfast $8.75, lunch $10.75, and dinner $18.75

VI'S RESTAURANT
808.871-6494
At the Maui Seaside Hotel. Great breakfast $5.00.
Dinner $8.00.

MARCO'S GRILL AND DELI
808.877-4446
Corner of Daisy Rd. and Hana Hwy. Breakfast $6.95, Lunch $5 - $10, Dinner $15 - $20.

ICHIBAN
808.871-6977
Kahului Shopping Center. Breakfast $6.00, Lunch $5 - $7, Dinner $12 - $20.

S.W. BARBECUE
Indoor/outdoor restaurant at the Maui Mall. Corner of Kaahumanu St. and Hana Hwy. Great Korean kal-bi, teriyaki, and chicken. Plate lunches under $5.00.

SAENG'S
808.244-1567
2119 Vineyard St. Thai food which can be spicy.
$5 - $15. Very pleasant setting in a garden with a waterfall.

SIAM THAI
808.244-3817
123 N. Market St. Great vegetarian meals. $5 - $15.

TASTY CRUST RESTAURANT
808.244-0845
1770 Mill St. Breakfast, Lunch, and Dinner. $6 - $15.

RAMON'S MEXICAN RESTAURANT
808.244-7243
2101 Vineyard St. Breakfast, Lunch, and Dinner. $5 - $10

In Kihei there are several satisfying pit stops for foodies. Look for the International House of Pancakes, also Denny's in the Kamaole Shopping Center. One restaurant you really should try in Upcountry Maui is

CASANOVA'S
808.572-0220
1188 Makawao Ave.

This is an Italian restaurant with maybe the best food you've ever tasted. A 10. Main courses $8 - $23. Whole pizzas start at $10. Lunch and Dinner. Dinner reservations are recommended. Deli is open all day.

BEST BEACHES

Maui's beaches are world class and numerous (eighty-one to be exact!). This means that as you are driving along you are highly tempted to stop the car and jump in for a dip. Most are easily accessible, with excellent swimming and bodysurfing.

A word of caution - many are open ocean beaches without reef protection. Some are safe for swimming. Others have rip currents all the time, or during winter's heavy surf or kona storms. Ask around. How safe is it? Don't swim alone.

In 1999 there were six shark attacks in Hawaii. All were on the outer islands. It's probably true that statistically you have a greater chance of being injured in an auto accident than being attacked by a shark. But statistics are small comfort if you're the victim. Ocean swimming in Hawaii is a lot safer than swimming in other areas such as Australia, Fiji, Tahiti.

TIP: I'd avoid swimming at Olowalu and Kahana Bay. I've seen some fins patrolling out that way.

KAMAOLE BEACHES I, II, AND III
2500 S. Kihei Rd.

These are extremely popular beach parks with restrooms and showers, picnic tables, barbecue grills, and paved parking lots. Wonderful whale watching in winter.

POLO, WAILEA, ULUA, MOKAPU AND KEAWAKAPU

In Wailea. (There are five great beaches in Wailea). Good bodysurfing and snorkeling. Crystal clear water. Watch out for Mokapu Beach in a high surf. Polo Beach was formerly known as Ferkany Beach. Wailea Beach is a long, lovely strip of sand backed by high dunes. Good snorkeling.

PALAUEA BEACH

Quite isolated. Follow the shoreline to the north side of Haloa Point and you'll come upon this stretch of sand which is largely deserted. Good swimming and bodysurfing, but dangerous in winter.

KAANAPALI BEACH

Wonderful beach fronting the entire resort complex.

KAPALUA BEACH

Also known as Fleming Beach. Next to the Kapalua Hotel. SAFEST SWIMMING BEACH, especially in winter.

HOOKIPA BEACH

On the Hana Hwy. Just a few miles from Kahului near Paia town.
World famous for surfing and windsurfing only. In winter swells reach 10 -15 feet high. Watch the action from the parking lot. For skilled, talented athletes.

HAMOA BEACH

In Hana, fronting the Hotel Hana Maui. Good surfing and bodysurfing. Watch out for rip currents.

There. That should keep you busy.

GETTING HERE

Just follow the suggestion regarding airlines and shipping household goods as described in this book. The only difference here is that you and your belongings will be routed from Honolulu to the port of Kahului, Maui. Maui No Ka Oe

(Maui is the best) as many islanders say - if you can afford it.

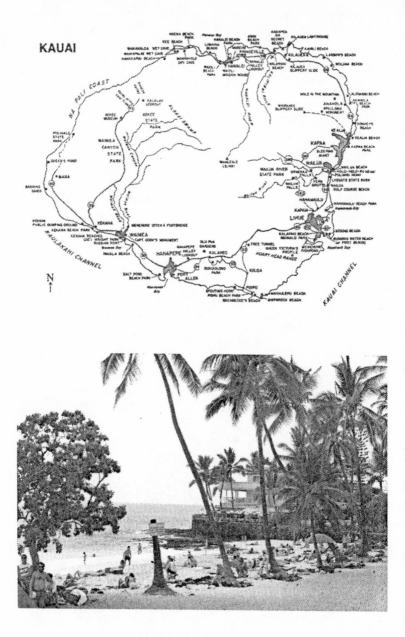

CHAPTER 4. KAUAI, THE GARDEN ISLAND

Kauai, the most Northern island in the Hawaiian chain, is the jewel of the string according to many Island lovers. Among those who know the Islands best there is no unanimity of opinion on this; each has his favorite and is willing to argue the point.

I first became enamored of Kauai years ago. We stayed at the Coco Palms Hotel, which faces the ocean and is set in a grove of a thousand coco palms. I remember being intrigued by a giant clam shell which served as a bathroom basin. Of such minutiae are memories made!

Pareu clad native boys blew huge conch shells to summon us to dinner. We strolled along winding paths lit by flickering torch lights. The sound of soft Hawaiian music filled the air. Hoo boy, it's hard to think of Kauai without waxing lyrical! And those Mai Tai's (fruit filled rum drinks) were the greatest!

CRIME FREE?

There's not much of a population on the island, and just one road around it, so violent crime is not a concern. A few burglaries, some pot-smoking, and domestic arguments are the norm. You can still sleep soundly at night in middle-class residential neighborhoods.

THE WEATHER

Weather reports on all of the islands typically intone: "Fair and sunny weather today with winds at fifteen miles per hour drifting mauka (from the mountains) to makai (toward the ocean). Tonight will be fair with occasional showers." Thus, the announcer reports on the most monotonously gorgeous daily weather in the world.

Kauai seems a bit cooler than the other islands with temperatures hovering between the sixties and the eighties.

Rainfall is heavy in winter through April, summer is hot and humid, September and October clear and sunny. Remember, while it may be raining in one spot, follow the sun and in a few minutes it may be clear as a bell!

In summer it's warm and humid in Princeville at Hanalei Bay on the North coast of Kauai. At the same time it's hot and dry in Poipu on the Southern shore. The weather tends to be cooler in Central Kauai. Mt. Waialeale is noted for being one of the wettest spots on earth - 400 to 500 inches of annual rainfall. The weather on the coastal beaches is generally pleasant and balmy. However, on the North Shore you may have to batten down the hatches during winter storms. Every decade or so one of these storms turns into a hurricane. The hurricanes seem to sneak around the southern coast of the Big Island, curving clockwise, then crashing into Kauai. The island is still recovering from the disastrous effects of Hurricane Iniki which hit in August, 1992.

COST OF LIVING AND JOB SITUATION

Unless you're in one of the construction trades , in a tourist-related business, or a professional, Kauai's jobs are few and far between. The cost of living is not as high as on Maui. Real estate sales and rental prices fell after Iniki, and now is a good time to purchase a condo or home at a fairly reasonable price. Condos range from $100,000 to $350,000, depending on location. Homes range from about $125,000 on up. The housing market is certainly more reasonable than on Maui. Rentals are slightly less, but food prices are high here also--higher than on the Big Island, and on a par with Maui. The cost of living is slightly less than on Maui because of cheaper housing, but you'd still need close to $2,000 per month income for basic expenses.

For information on local rentals, write for a subscription to:

The Garden Isle
P. O. Box 231
Lihue, Kauai 96766
Phone: (808) 245-3681

WHAT'S IT LIKE?

NORTH SHORE -(Na Pali Coast, Princeville, Hanalei Bay, Lumahai Beach)

Kauai's North Shore, which includes the breathtaking Na Pali Coast, Princeville, Hanalei Bay, and Lumahai Beach (site of the movie "South Pacific") has to be some of the most spectacular scenery on planet Earth.

Plan on viewing the Na Pali Coast from May through October. Unpredictable winter storms and high surf with waves rising fifteen or twenty feet high make small craft and rubber raft trips unsafe during winter months.

These spectacular cliffs have been filmed in at least twenty-five motion pictures, including the beautiful waterfall scene in Jurassic Park. You can hike the cliffs, or view them from sailboats or rubber rafts. The zodiac rides commence from Tunnels Beach on the Northeast or from Southwest Kekaha. It's an unforgettable trip. Green sea turtles and porpoises swim alongside the raft.

Cave formations are carved into the sheer cliffs. You can ride right into the caves, where shafts of sunlight turn the sea into a transparent, eerie undersea cathedral. Visitors actually gasp at the waterfalls and magnificent changing colors of sea and sky.

Lumahai is actually not a huge beach, just a mile and a quarter of soft powder sand perfect for a solitary ride on horseback, or a jog into the surf. Its spectacular beauty stems from the backdrop of a mountain cliff and the everchanging pastel play of colors framing the beach. The golden orb of the sun sends shafts of light across the cliffs ranging from violet to blue, pink, orange and green. Fluffy white clouds drift overhead and a rainbow arches across the sky. There are only one or two people on the beach. You wonder if this is real and wish you could freeze this moment in memory.

Hanalei Bay is best viewed from the terrace of the Princeville Resort Hotel. Be sure to bring your camera. The panoramic scene is breathtaking. It's an unforgettable experience, beautiful in any weather, rain or shine.

Nearby Princeville is a self-contained community built around its world-class golf courses. Years ago it was a cattle ranch. Now cliffside villas, hotels, and condominiums overlook the beach. It's a mighty nice environment, but as you would expect, prices are upscale.

CENTRAL KAUAI-KAPAA AND LIHUE

An unbroken ribbon of sand stretches for nearly three miles between the Wailua and Hanamaulu rivers, paralleling the Municipal Golf Course and sugar cane fields. High waves make swimming hazardous, and the beach is nearly deserted except for a few skilled swimmers and divers, and an occasional fisherman. You can still find glass balls that have floated in from Japanese fishing boats. In the vicinity of Lihue and Kapaa are most of the island's residential neighborhoods. Here you can find reasonable rental prices.

POIPU

The Southeastern section of the island has probably the best climate, dry and sunny. Beaches, golf courses, and scenery are spectacular. This area is extremely desirable living, but as you would expect, real estate costs are high.

Overall, Kauai's towering cliffs and rolling surf crashing against the rocks, its green hills and valleys, its spun sugar beaches and cool breezes can clutch your heart. But - when you think about living there - consider also that it's quite a small island, and the shopping facilities that you take for granted on the mainland are not available. Locals plan shopping trips occasionally to Honolulu's Ala Moana Shopping Center, especially at Christmas.

In fact, Waikiki Hotels advertise special discounted rates for outer island shoppers during the Christmas season.

Let's zero in on affordable lodging, reasonable restaurants, and best beaches:

LODGING

Hotels on Kauai, as on Maui, tend to be pricey - that is $200 to $500 per night. Your best bet is to stay at a B &B - average price $60 per night. Contact the following agencies for listings:

> BED & BREAKFAST HAWAII
> 800.733-1632
> 6436 Kalama Rd., Kapaa, Hi. 96746
> Range $50 - $150
>
> BED & BREAKFAST KAUAI
> 800.822-1176
>
> POIPU BED & BREAKFAST
> 800.552-0095

These agencies will require a deposit to hold your reservation, and may require a minimum stay of 2 - 3 nights. You'll need to book 2 - 3 months in advance. On all of the islands accommodations are in great demand during the winter season of December through April.

CAMPING

Although all of the islands offer camping through the State's Department of Land & Natural Resources, camping on Kauai is particularly appealing and inexpensive.

KOKEE LODGE
808.335-6061
Box 819, Waimea, Hi. 96796

Rent a cabin fully equipped with stove, refrigerator, hot shower, kitchen utensils, bedding, and wood burning stove for $35 - $45 night.

Maximum stay is five nights. The Kokee wilderness area is lovely but at a high elevation. Bring sweaters and jackets.

Y.M.C.A. CAMP NAUE
Y.M.C.A. of Kauai
P. O. Box 1786, Lihue, Hi. 96766

Beachfront camping at beautiful Haena on the North Shore in bunk houses or your own tent.

A bunk costs $16 per night.

RESTAURANTS

KOLOA BROILER
808.742-9122

Located in the center of Old Koloa Town in Poipu.

A real find. Loaded with funky atmosphere. The least expensive steak house on Kauai. Broil your own, plus baked beans, salad, and bread $11.95.

Other items on the menu such as kabobs and fish are equally reasonable. Open 11 am to 10 pm.

KEOKI'S
808.742-7534

In Poipu Shopping Village. Dinner only. Very popular. Reservations a must. Varied menu from lassagna to prime rib. $9.95 to $19.95. Tasty food. Try their hula pie.

KALAHEO STEAK HOUSE
808.322-9780
4444 Papalino Rd.

No reservations taken. Dinner only. Chicken, ribs, steak, prime rib. Excellent food. $12.95 - $22.95

BRENNECKE'S BEACH BROILER
808.742-7588

Across the street from Poipu Beach. Specializing in fresh fish. Lunch - salad bar plus sandwiches, burgers, and fish. Dinner can be reasonable (salad bar and clam chowder) $10.95. Barbecue ribs $16.95, and fresh island fish expertly broiled $19.95. Dinner reservations a must. Very popular.

TIP TOP RESTAURANT
Lihue. 3173 Akahi St.

Open daily except Mondays at 6:45 a.m.
Terrific breakfasts. $4.50 - $5.50. Pancakes, omelettes, pork chops.

KOUNTRY KITCHEN
808.822-3511
Kapaa. 1485 Kuhio Hwy.
Breakfast and lunch 6 am - 2:30 pm
Try their omelettes. Best breakfast on the island.
Breakfast $6.00 Lunch $6 - $8.

KALAPAKI BEACH HUT
808.246-3464
Lihue. 3464 Rice St. on Kalapaki Bay.
Kauai's best hamburgers. $3.75 - $5.50.
Wide variety of burgers.

HANAMAULU RESTAURANT
808.245-2511
Rt. 56

Lunch and Dinner. 35 different Oriental entrees.
$4.75 - $14.75. Adjacent tea house. Reservations a must. A very special place where the food is beautifully prepared and served.

HAMURA'S SAIMIN
Lihue. 2956 Kress St. Cash only.
A landmark specializing in saimin. $4.25.

Try their lilikoi (passion fruit) pie. It's ono.

CHUCK'S STEAK HOUSE
808.826-6211
Hanalei at the Princeville Center.
Lunch and Dinner. Over 25 entrees.
Excellent luncheon fare $5.95 - $8.95.
Dinner $13.75 - $24.50. No sensational views, just reasonable, well-prepared meals.

Kauai is peppered with fast food eateries, bakeries that serve sandwiches also, and health food bars. Try Papaya's Garden Café in the Kauai Village Shopping Center, Wailua) for fresh fruits, salads, and muffins.

In closing, there is an extraordinary restaurant with exceptional atmosphere that I'd like to mention. If you're willing and able to shell out a few more dollars for a memorable dining experience, don't miss Gaylord's at Kilohana.

Easier on the pocketbook for lunch ($6.95 - $10) than dinner, for dinner entrees are all over $20.

GAYLORD'S
808.245-9593
Rt. 50, west of Lihue.

What makes Gaylord's memorable is its unique setting. Once the manor house of a 1,700 acre sugar plantation, the restaurant has supplanted the dining room and spacious veranda of the original home of Gaylord Wilcox, its owner. Walking out on to the flagstone terrace is like stepping back in time to a more elegant and leisurely lifestyle. You'll dine with white linen on the table, attentive waiters to serve you, madam, while you inhale the scent of sweet gardenias from the fragrant garden. Food's good, too. The rest of the house has been converted into interesting gift shops and a Hawaiiana art gallery. If you'd enjoy a romantic experience with your spouse or a date, remember Gaylord's.

BEST BEACHES

KALAPAKI BEACH
Fronts the Marriott Hotel , Lihue. Park at the hotel parking lot off Rice St. Great swimming and boogie boarding. All of Kauai's beaches are subject to high surf warnings in winter months, so watch out for the big waves that can come out of nowhere and slam you. The trick is to dive under the wave before it hits.

LYDGATE PARK
Next to the Wailua Golf Course. Very safe swimming for children and toddlers year round.

Natural rock pools for snorkeling. Great swimming, showers, and usually a lifeguard on duty.

ANAHOLA BAY
Rt. 56. Turn off at Aliomanu Road and follow it to the end.

Another wonderful family beach. Safest at the north end where the stream flows into the sea. Good boogie boarding. At certain times of the year jellyfish come in at all of the beaches so be wary.

If you see any "man o'war" floating in the water or on the sand, make a hasty exit.

HANALEI BAY
Fronts the Princeville Hotel.

So spectacular it defies description and inspires musical compositions. Great for swimming in the summer, but high surf in the winter.

KALIHIWAI BAY
Take Rt. 56 north.

Great family beach, but not for wintertime swimming. Nearly all of the beaches on the north shore can be dangerous in the winter with high surf and rip currents.

TUNNELS BEACH
Take Rt. 560 pass the 8 mile marker and the YMCA camp. No parking lot.

Large lagoon protected by two reefs which makes for safe swimming even in winter months.

Great for snorkeling.

POIPU BEACH PARK
Across from Brennecke's Beach Broiler
on Hoone Road.

Absolutely perfect for children, toddlers, and grownups. Sugar sand and lava rock pools.

Walk or swim on down in front of the Waiohai Hotel and feed the fish frozen peas. Great snorkeling.

LUMAHAI BEACH
Rt. 560 just past the 4 mile marker.

The movie "South Pacific" was filmed here.

Incredibly beautiful. No reef protection.

Stay very close to shore. Rip tides and high surf.

At its west end an ice cold stream flows into the sea. Use it to rinse off.

Kauai's beaches are too numerous to mention here. There's something for everyone. Even a nudist beach (Secret Beach). Where is it?

Take Rt. 56 North. Turn right on Kalihwai Road,

Beyond the first curve, turn right on a dirt road to the end. Park and lock your car. Follow the trail to the bottom. Who knows what you'll find? I leave that to your imagination.

The longest beach on all of the islands, about twenty-five miles long, lies along the base of the Na Pali Cliffs, largely accessible only by boat or by hiking in - not recommended unless you have a seasoned guide and are in top condition.

GETTING HERE

Just follow the suggestions in the chapter on the Mechanics of Moving, except that you and your belongings will be routed from Honolulu to the Port of Nawiliwili, Kauai.

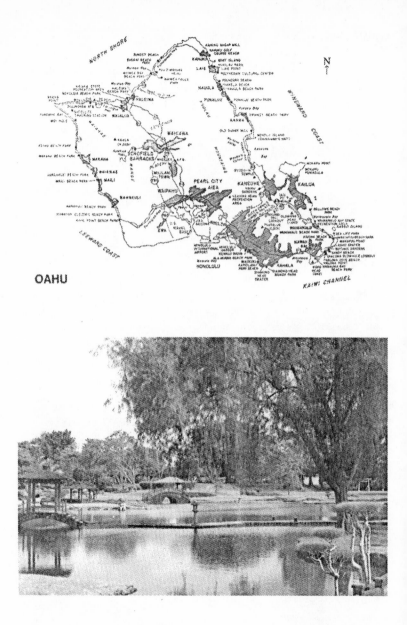

OAHU

CHAPTER 5. OAHU, THE GATHERING PLACE

Since land on Oahu is scarce- it doesn't have the wide open spaces of the Big Island - and demand for land is great, Oahu until recently was very expensive. However, the recent recession and Hawaii's economic downturn has resulted in a renter's market in housing. This has made Oahu living more affordable in 2000 than it has been in many years. It's opened up a window of opportunity for many to experience island living.

WHAT'S IT LIKE?

The Oahu of yesteryear was an incredibly beautiful island, where life proceeded at a slow, langorous pace. The addition of miles of concrete, a million cars, and skyscrapers, has changed the face of the island. Today, the city of Honolulu is a hustling, bustling metropolis, home to eight hundred thousand people.

It's evolved into an exciting town with wonderful shopping, entertainment, and restaurants of every ethnic flavor. Local people have always loved music and parties, and take every opportunity to celebrate, whether it be for a baby's first birthday luau (party), or to celebrate long deceased Prince Kuhio's birthday. In fact, if you add the State of Hawaii holidays to the Federal holidays, you have quite a few days off to celebrate.

And islanders have every reason to celebrate each day. For Oahu is still beautiful, with balmy breezes caressing your skin, brilliant blue skies and puffy white clouds drifting overhead. The island is ringed with palm fringed beaches and white crested waves rolling toward shore with methodic military precision If you're fortunate enough to spend a year or two on Oahu, in later years you'll cherish memories of a very special time and place.

Oahu is so special, that natives who have left its shores and lived on the mainland U.S. for forty years, are moved to tears when they hear the strains of Hawaiian music. Their hearts fill with longing and yearn to return to the smiling faces and sweet kindnesses known worldwide as "Aloha."

I have to interject here that this longing may be nostalgia for a kinder, gentler way of life. During the past ten years Honolulu has been wrestling with problems that plague other large cities on the mainland. Traffic jams, burglaries, purse snatching, and the latest shock -graffiti defacing cemeteries. Honolulu has never experienced anything remotely like that before. Residents are outraged. A large reward has been offered to find the culprits. Book 'em, Danno. Over seven hundred people volunteered to clean up the red paint.

THE WEATHER

The weather is incomparable, ranging from the seventies to the nineties in summer. Because of all of the concrete poured on the island, it seems hotter in recent years. On Oahu, as on the other islands, there's an astounding variety of microclimates on the island. Mt. Kaala, in the Waianae range, at 4,050 feet above sea level, is the highest spot on the island. If you prefer a cooler climate, head for the cool, green hills that bisect the island.

GEOGRAPHY

Before we start around the island, let's look at our map. If you turn it on its side, the shape of the island sort of looks like a wolf's head. It has four coastlines: the North Shore, the Windward side of the island comprising the bedroom communities of Kailua and Kaneohe, the Waianae Coast from Barber's Point to Kaena Point, and the Southern Coast, from Pearl Harbor south. Two mountain ranges split the island, the Waianae range and the Koolaus. Between the two ranges lie the central valley lowlands.

Rainfall is heavy in the hills and sparse on the lowlands. Prevailing tradewinds blow from Northwest to Southeast. Windward Oahu is lush and green, as are the leeward valleys of Palolo, Manoa, Nuuanu, and Kalihi.

Waikiki is almost an island by itself, with the Ala Wai Canal on its East, and the Pacific Ocean on its Western shore. Metropolitan Honolulu is often described as America's most beautiful city with its open spaces, its parks, and its colorful flowering trees.

Then there is rural Oahu, which is like a neighbor island - much slower pace, deserted beaches, green rolling hills, waterfalls, and sleepy little towns dozing in the sun. C'mon, Pueo, I'm glad you got here just in time to take a trip around the island with me, starting with

WAIKIKI

Diamond Head, an extinct volcano, borders the beach on the South, and Ala Moana beach park on its North. Waikiki Beach is only a short strip of land, but some of the finest resort hotels in the world are just footsteps away, amid many thriving businesses in high-rise office buildings.

Waikiki is urban Honolulu. Bright city lights reflect off the ocean at night. Tourists throng its streets by day and the ambience is one of both relaxation and excitement. Coconut palms sway in breezes redolent with the smell of perfumed plumeria. Strains of soft Hawaiian music linger in the air. At night Waikiki pulses with the rhythm of guitars and drums while the hips of hula dancers swivel to the beat.

The beach is incomparable. Sugar sand stretching for miles along the shore. What really makes the beach splendid is the temperature of the water - near perfect seventy degrees year round, and the perfect wave action. So measured. Great waves for body surfing, canoeing, or surfboarding. Swimmers, take note. Waikiki is about the safest beach in Hawaii. It's surrounded by a protective reef.

Waikiki has always been and still is a great place to live. Super convenience - you're surrounded by shops and estaurants. The downside - it's noisy! Garbage trucks clanging early in the morning, the noise of cars, and it's crowded with tourists. So, if you like peace and solitude, Waikiki is not the place for you. Pueo says he prefers

ALA MOANA

It seems that everybody, young or old, sooner or later visits Ala Moana. The largest shopping center on the island, with over two hundred stores, it draws both residents and visitors like a magnet.

The shopping center is bordered by the Kapiolani corridor of high rise residential and office condos, which offer a very convenient location and moderate rents.

A great attraction in this area besides the shopping center, is the proximity of Ala Moana Beach Park. Locals definitely prevail, while the tourists congregate in Waikiki. Thousands of local kids have learned to swim in the smooth waters inside the reef, On any given day you'll see thousands of people engaged in surfing, tennis, football, in-line skating, croquet, flying kites, and lawn bowling. Hobbyists race remote controlled airplances, sailboats, and hydroplanes on the lagoon at the Waikiki end of the beach, and exercise clubs are hard at work making mere spectators feel guilty.

When he saw those wahines huffing and. puffing, Pueo commented that I ought to join them. How rude. He reads my mind sometimes, that bird. I was planning a trip to the Yum Yum Tree for their English toffee pie until he made that remark. I told him I'm getting tired of his putdowns and he should look at his own beer belly!

Pueo said to tell you that if you like the action, you'd enjoy living at Ala Moana. Even if you don't participate, it's entertaining just to people watch.

SOUTHEAST

We hopped into my little Honda that I keep at my condo at the Wailana for a ride to see how the rich and famous live. I love the Wailana. All you have to do is take the elevator down to that wonderful coffee shop downstairs.

(Occasionally I'd ride the elevator along with Wilt "The Stilt" Chamberlain who owned a penthouse in the building). But, guess what? The Wailana has had a bunch of Hondas stolen right out of their parking garage lately. Thank goodness mine wasn't one of them, or we wouldn't be taking this trip!

Along the shoreline from Diamond Head, through Kahala, Niu Valley, Kuliouou, Hawaii Kai and on to Makapuu, I have only one comment to make - EXPENSIVE. The homes and neighborhoods are just beautiful, but if you're on a budget, this is not for you. This also applies to the hills along this route - St. Louis Heights, Wilhelmina Rise, Waialae Iki, Waialae Ridge, and the hills in Hawaii Kai.

There's just one residential area in this section where you might find reasonable apartment rentals, and that's in Kaimuki. Pueo insisted that we stop in Kaimuki for his favorite brew, before heading over the Pali to the

WINDWARD SIDE

Driving down the Pali highway through the tunnel is probably the most scenic drive on the island. When you emerge from the tunnel and see the sparkling waters of Kailua Bay below, it takes your breath away. Even Pueo, the cynic, blurted "Wow! What a view!" as we descended the Pali highway.

Windward Oahu extends from Kahuku on the North to Waimanalo on the South end of the island, and encompasses several bedroom communities, the small towns of Mormon Laie with its Polynesian Cultural Center, through Punaluu, Kaaawa, Kaneohe, Kailua, Lanikai, and lastly Waimanalo. (Don't worry, the Hawaiian place names aren't so hard after you get used to them. All it takes is repetition).

We didn't tarry long in Kaneohe, because Pueo complained that he had a stomach ache, he was so hungry. I said, "Okay, we'll stop and see if we can find you a gecko out on the North Shore."

NORTH SHORE

The North Shore extends from the Kaena Point Lighthouse, past Mokuleia, Haleiwa, and Waimea Bay to Sunset Beach. It's a spectacularly beautiful coastline, particularly in winter, when the giant waves crest at Makaha. Here you can find inexpensive housing, because it is a sixty to ninety drive to metropolitan Honolulu.

We sped along Kam Highway and decided to stop for lunch at Pat's at Punaluu. I had a kalua pig sandwich and fresh fruit. Pueo spotted a fat gecko sunbathing on a rock. Scratch one gecko! He said he wanted to try a Mexican imported beer for a change (Dos Equis - two x's), and burped his approval.

Pat's is a favorite pit stop. Their dinner menu features glazed guava lamb, shimp curry, and chocolate macadamia nut pie! Boy, we better get on our way. What a temptation to spend the afternoon on the beach and stay for dinner! After dessert, Pueo was so sleepy he dozed all the way to the central valleys.

CENTRAL VALLEYS

These are a series of bedroom communities for Honolulu. Starting on the North at Wahiawa, adjacent to Schofield Barracks, you drop down to Wheeler Air Force Base, Mililani, Pearl City, Aiea, and Salt Lake. At Pearl City, there's a junction on the H-1 freeway through Waipahu and Ewa Beach.

Housing is moderately priced in the Central Valleys, particularly in Wahiawa which is very green, cool, and beautiful. This is a noteworthy area to go house hunting. Mililani is also a good bet. Mililani is a planned community with a private golf club, and homes are pricey, yet there are some affordable townhouses for rent. The same is true for Pearl City, Aiea, Salt Lake, Waipahu, and Ewa Beach.

By this time Pueo was slightly tipsy and getting restless, so I told him, "You'd better go on home while it's still daylight. But be careful. The cops are out in full force looking for DUI's."

Pueo nodded assent, but he could barely make it off the ground. Once airborne, he dipped his left wing in a salute, then zoomed toward the Koolaus.

We've just completed our armchair tour of the island. Now that you are somewhat familiar with the terrain, let's take a look at housing costs and availability.

HOUSING AVAILABILITY AND COST

Your housing cost is a key factor in being able to afford living on Oahu. Reflecting Hawaii's downturn during the recent recession, **it's a renter's market on Oahu in 2000.** Just a short time ago, renters struggled to find an available condo to rent, often being placed on a waiting list, and rents were very high for both houses and condominiums.

Today, landlords are now more willing to offer a price break, or even offer an incentive such as two weeks of free rent to fill an apartment.

What's caused the 180 degree turnaround? The number of available rental units is way up primarily beause of three factors:

1. Competition from subsidized local government housing. The military has built so many housing units that armed forces personnel now live on base.
2. Construction of new housing units has declined substantially in recent recession years.
3. While the economy has recovered in many areas on the mainland, Hawaii's economy is still in the doldrums.

RENTING A HOUSE

The median rent asked for all homes on Oahu dropped from $1,100 in 1993 to $1,000 in 1996. This means that half of the homes are below that asking price and half are above. Does that mean that there is today a glut of rental homes on the market? Not so.

Bear in mind that the median cost of a home on Oahu today is in the $330,000 range, and you will realize instantly that there are many more condos available for rent than there are houses, and that you're not going to be able to rent a $330,000 home for anywhere near $1,000 per month. The owner probably has a sizable mortgage and would drown in a negative cash flow at that rental. The $1,000 per month rental houses will be very small older homes located at least one hour's drive from the city.

Therefore, if you're on a shoestring budget, unless you're willing to share a house, renting a condo is your best bet.

SHARING ACCOMMODATIONS

The **Honolulu Advertiser** has a lengthy section in the Classfieds under Rentals to Share. You would have to interview your prospective roomates to find a congenial situation. Keep in mind that entering into a living arrangement with strangers can be risky. A personal recommendation would be the better route.

The University of Hawaii and the Y.M.C.A./Y.W.C.A.will also have bulletin boards advertising rooms and shared accommodations for rent.

RENTING A CONDO

In 2000, there is a glut of rental condos on Oahu. It definitely is a renter's market. Renting a condo is vastly more affordable than renting a home, and has the added advantage of better security, particularly in a high rise building. With eight hundred thousand people milling around today on the island, pesonal security and possible burglary issues need to be considered.

If you decide to try a low-rise condominium, look for a gated community that is patrolled and where you can keep a watchdog. An alarm system is recommended for your car, or get "The Club" for your car steering wheel, as auto theft is big business on Oahu. Better yet, get a car which has an electronic chip embedded in the key without which thieves can't start the car. Great idea - it'll take awhile for thieves to figure out a way around that one!

The average rental price for a one bedroom partially furnished (appliances, drapes, carpet) condo on Oahu in 2000 is $800 per month, $100 less than the rental price in 1993. **Rental costs for a one bedroom are as low as $600 per month in some areas.** Rentals in a high rise are significantly less than in a townhome or home.

LOCATING A REASONABLE RENTAL

Tracking the housing rental ads in the Sunday Honolulu Star-Bulletin/Advertiser is your best bet. You can have the Sunday paper mailed to you by writing to:

Honolulu Advertiser
605 Kapiolani Blvd.
Honolulu, Hi. 96814
(808) 539-8517

A typical Sunday rental ad section contains an inventory of about thirty-five furnished homes, and about four hundred partially furnished condos.

If you're a single or a married couple without young children, high rise living can be a great experience and carefree living. Young children simply do not adapt well to high rise living. The issue is safety. Toddlers have fallen to their deaths from high-rise lanais. Families with older children adjust more readily to apartment conveniences.

The benefits are super convenience, with restaurants and shopping centers within walking distance, beautiful views of mountains and the ocean, incredible sunsets, security, no yard work, and bugs are a lot easier to control. Most buildings have recreation centers and offer a recreation floor, tennis court, swimming pool, and/or putting green.

High rise residents in **Waikiki, Kailua, and Aiea** particularly love nearby shopping, restaurants, movies, night life, and short drives to work.

Apartments in the Waikiki/Kapiolani/ Ala Moana area tend to be furnished. Rentals range from studios at $550 to $650, one bedrooms from $800 to $900, and two bedrooms from $1200 to $1500. This area is more expensive because of the popularity of Waikiki Beach and Ala Moana Beach Park.

If you're willing to drive a half hour to an hour, you can find a nice, partially furnished two bedroom in Aiea for $750 - $800. The Windward side of the island offers many apartments at reasonable rates. So does the North Shore (Makaha, Haleiwa,

Waialua), and the Central Valley from Wahiawa South. If you're on a tight budget, a high rise is the way to go.

LODGING UPON ARRIVAL

The dilemma of where to stay when you arrive is easily solved. Tell your moving company that you will let them know where to ship your belongings. They'll allow you a grace period, usually thirty days, to find a permanent address. After that, they'll charge you for placing your household goods in storage.

LOW COST HOTELS

If you want to stay in a hotel when you arrive, bargains are not to be found on popular beaches or near eighteen hotel golf courses. The best selection for clean and reputable bargain hotels are found on Oahu.

Following is a list of recommended low cost hotels:

INN ON THE PARK
1920 Ala Moana Blvd., Waikiki
1-800-445-6633, Range $67 - $100

ISLAND COLONY
445 Seaside Ave., Waikiki
1-800-854-8843, Range $60 - $135

KOBAYASHI HOTEL
(808) 536-2277
250 N. Beretania St., Downtown
Budget hotel - $25 per night

PAGODA HOTEL
1525 Rycroft St., near Ala Moana
1-800-367-6060. Locals love to
stay here. The thousands of koi carp
are worth the price of admission.
Range $54 to $85. Highly recommended.

OTHER COST OF LIVING FACTORS

FOOD

Since you may be living in a high-rise, you won't be able to grow your own fruits and vegetables as in a home on one of the neighbor islands. The trick to keep your food costs down is to hit the local farmer's markets which are held once a week in rotating neighborhoods. You can find a superior variety of fresh fruits and vegetables at prices 30% to 40% less than local supermarket prices. Here's the scoop on keeping food costs down:

Oahu Market. Chinatown landmark collection of shops and stalls offers bargains on produce, meats, and fish, especially ingredients for Asian recipes. Street parking only. Try the bus. 6 a.m. to 3 p.m. Monday - Saturday. 6 a.m. to noon Sunday. 145 N. King St. Information: 841-6924.

Honolulu Farmer's Market. 404 Piikoi St. Locally harvested produce, plants, flowers, and seafood. Park free on adjacent lot. 6 a.m. - noon Saturday and Sunday. Information: 522-7088. The schedule:

Monday. 6:45 - 7:45 a.m. at **Manoa Valley District Park,** 2721 Kaaipu Ave., 8:30 - 9:30 a.m. at **Makiki District Park** on Keeaumoku St. 10:00 - 11:15 a.m. at **Mother Waldron Park,** 525 Coral St., 11:45 a.m. - 12:30 pm.at **City Hall parking lot deck**. Alapai and Beretania Sts.

Tuesday -6:30 to 7:30 a.m. at **Waiau District Park**, 98-1650 Kaahumanu St., Pearl City. 8:15 a.m. to 9:15 a.m. at **Waipahu District Park,** 94-230 Paiwa St., 10 - 11 a.m.at **Wahiawa District Park,** North Cane St. and California Ave.

Wednesday - 6:30 to 730 a.m. at Palolo Valley District Park, 2007 Palolo Ave., 8:15 - 9:15 a.m.at **McCully District**

Park, 831 Pumehana St., 10 - 11:00 a.m. at **Kapiolani Park,** Monsarrat and Paki Ave.

Thursday - 7:15 - 8:15 a.m. at **Waimanalo Beach Park,** 41-741 Kalanianiole Hwy., 9 - 10:00 a.m. at **Kailua District Park,** 21 S. Kainalu Dr., 10:45 a.m. to 11:45 a.m. at **Kaneohe District Park,** 45-660 Keahala Road.

Friday - 7 - 8:00 a.m.at **Aiea District Park,** 99-350 Aiea Heights Drive. 9 - 10:00 a.m. at **Ewa Beach Community Park,** 91-955 North Road, 11 - 11:45 a.m. at **Pokai Bay Beach Park,** 85-037 Pokai Bay Road.

Saturday - 6:15 - 7:30 a.m. at **Banyan Court Mall, 800 N. King St., 8:15 - 9:30 a.m.** at Kauumualii Street and 700 Kalihi St., 10 - 10:45 a.m. at **Kalihi Valley District Park**, 1911 Kamehameha IV Road.   11:15 a.m. -noon at **Salt Lake Municipal Lot,** 5337 Likini St., 1-2:00 p.m. at **Hawaii Kai Park-n-Ride,** 300 Keahole St.

There you have it! One or more of these farmer's markets will be located close to your condo, and if you make the effort to buy food there, you'll not only enjoy the freshest fruits, produce, and fish, you'll slice your grocery bill by about 35%!

BREAD

Love's Bakery has an outlet at 870 Kapahulu Ave. that sells marvelous day-old loaves and pastries at huge discounts Additional seniors 10% discounts on Tuesdays and Fridays. Although you may pay $3.50 for a loaf at the supermarket, you can buy it here for $1.49. Call information - 737-5564.

Other outlets: **Aiea store,** 99-080 Kauhale St., information 487-1612. **Downtown store,** 66 S. Hotel St., information 545-1891. **Kaneohe store,** 46-028 Kawa St., information 235-5171. **Waipahu store,** 94-226 Leoku St., information 677-0423. All stores are open daily.

Holsum/Orowheat Thrift Store. Discounts are given on Wednesday and Saturday; seniors receive an additional 10% discount every day. Most stores are not open on Sundays. **Aiea store,** 98-150 Kaonihi St., information 488-1338. **Kalihi store,** 1810 N. King St.,information 841-2660. Not open Sunday. **Kailua Store,** 315 Uluniu St., information 261-9847. Not open Sunday. **Moiliili Store,** 2858 S. King St., information 941-3877.

Sometimes they'll give you a freebie. Doesn't hurt to ask!

MILK, EGGS, HONEY, AND SPECIALTY CHEESES

The cheapest milk is of course powdered, but it just doesn't taste as good as fresh. I use it for emergencies, and for cooking. Milk price increases are regulated by the State Dept. of Agriculture and have to be approved by the Governor! Milk costs are double that of mainland prices because of the cost of importing grain for cows. Or, at least that's the excuse given!

Other dairy products may be purchased directly from local farmers on the Windward and North Shores at a discount.

MEAT - POULTRY, BEEF, PORK

Much poultry is grown on the island and the price of chicken and turkey in the supermarkets is not particularly high. Frozen chicken legs sell for $1.00 per pound. As to supermarket prices, Safeway consistently offers good value.

MISCELLANEOUS - SOAP POWDER, CLEANSING SOLUTIONS, PAPER TOWELS, TOILET PAPER

These are best bought weekly in bulk from the discount houses Costco, Wal-Mart, or K-Mart who have helped to bring prices down in Hawaii.

Next to housing, buying food will be your biggest monthly expenditure. Learn to cook some Oriental stir-fry dishes, where your meat and vegetables are cut up instead of served in gigantic portions. Tasty and healthy with a diminished use of fat. Try steamed rice instead of potatoes. If you don't like it plain, experiment with adding pilaf style spices.

If you're careful with your shopping, and cook nutritious meals at home, two can eat for $350.00 per month. Add ice cream, strawberries, and desserts, and you're looking at $400.00 per month. Add a weekly dinner for two out at a moderately priced restaurant, and your food bill rises to $500 - $550 per month.

RESTAURANT MEALS FOR $10 OR LESS

AUNTIE PASTO'S
1099 S. Beretania St., in Makiki. Ph. 523-8855. Lunch and dinner, except for weekends dinner only. Everybody loves the Italian food here.

BANDITO'S CANTINA
Pearlridge Shopping Center, Aiea
Ph. 488-8888. Lunch and dinner daily.
Good Tex-Mex cooking. Tacos, enchiladas, chile rellenos and the whole nine yards. Delicioso.

THE OLIVE TREE
4614 Kilauea Ave., Kahala,
Ph. 737-0303. Greek food. Turkish, too. Fish, lamb, and chicken with baklava for dessert. Dinner only. Daily service.

PEOPLE'S CAFE
1300 Pali Hwy., Downtown Honolulu
Ph. 536-5789. Specializes in local fare, especially Hawaiian dishes such as kalua pig, lomilomi salmon, chicken luau or chicken with long rice. Laulaus and oxtail stew. Very filling. Lunch and dinner, Monday through Saturday.

A LITTLE BIT OF SAIGON
1160 Maunakea St., Downtown Honolulu

Ph. 528-3663. Vietnamese food, spicy but good. Try the spring rolls with minced fish. Lunch and dinner daily. No liquor served but bring your own bottle of beer or wine.

KRUNG THAI
1028 Nuuanu Ave., Downtown Honolulu
Ph. 599-4803. Marvelous food from Thailand. Try their chicken in various peanut and coconut milk sauces. Open only for lunch Monday through Friday. A real find.

IRIFUNE
563 Kapahulu Ave., near Waikiki
Ph. 737-1141. Japanese stir fry platters, tempura, sukiyaki, etc. Tuesday through Friday, lunch only.
Saturday and Sunday dinner only. BYOB.

INDIA BAZAAR MADRAS CAFE
2320 South King St., near the University
Ph. 949-4840. Indian curries, chutneys, samosas, marinated chicken. Lunch and dinner daily.

Honolulu has no shortage of ethnic eateries with low prices. Take a trip around the world without ever leaving the island. More of the same **Kin Wah Chop Suey,** Kaneohe. Ph. 247-4812. Delicious. Dinner for three - $15.00. **Mizutani Coffee Shop,** Ph. 597-8146. Former Benihana chef. Mini-plates $2.80, Regular plates $4.00. **Kenny's Burger House.** Ph. 841-4782 Kam Shopping Center in Kalihi. Local favorite. Feed six for under $10.00. **Bishop St. Cafe.** Ph. 537-6951. Great downtown lunches under $6.00. **Boston's North End Pizza,** Ph. 263-2253. Six stores. Lotsa pizza for a small price. **I Love Country Cafe.** Ph. 596-8108. Near Ala Moana. Health conscious food.

Others: **Victoria Inn, Columbia Inn, The Greek Corner, Kairyu, Zippy's, Kim Chee and L & L Drive Inn chains. Also, Rainboiw Drive-In and Byron's Drive-In.**

Just so you won't starve while on the island, you may also enjoy

FIVE DOLLAR PLATE LUNCHES

An Hawaiian tradition, the ubiquitous plate lunch is the mainstay of the working man or woman's diet. Heavy on the carbs though - two scoops of rice, potato-macaroni salad, and meat smothered with gravy is the mainstay. Some offer teriyaki steak, mahimahi on a bun, and/or beef curry.

These lunches now cost about $5.95 (inflation), but you get a whopper of a meal for the price. Hawaii's construction workers would faint without them. If you want to carbo down, look for the lunchwagons. Everyone has a favorite location. Mine for many years was the lunchwagon still parked at Fisherman's Wharf. Here are some to get you started:

MASU'S PLATE LUNCH
Corner of Liliha and Kuakini Sts. Try Paul's Massive Plate Lunch, but don't plan on doing anything else but sleeping afterward.

GRACE'S INN AND RAINBOW DRIVE INN.
Both in Kapahulu.

KENEKE'S PLATE LUNCH. Waimanalo.
Try their Kal-bi (Korean short ribs marinated in garlic, pepper, and shoyu).

AHI'S RESTAURANT. Kahuku.
For local color, you won't want to miss this. A big sign with an arrow on a broken down truck near the Kahuku Sugar Mill points the way. Slack key guitar and Hawaiian music on Friday nights.

Ask directions of local people and they'll be glad to help you find your way. Honolulu is loaded with truly elegant restaurants, but these nickel and dime establishments will help you afford an occasional splurge.

UTILITIES

Power bills on Oahu, as on the neighbor islands, are not bad even though thermal unit costs are high, because no heating is necessary and cool breezes provide ventilation even in summer. Ovens and washer/dryers are powered by either gas or electricity.

If you're in a high rise with central airconditioning, unless you're in a new building with energy conservation measures in place, your monthly power bill could run as much as $200 - $250. In cooler areas, such as Makiki or Salt Lake, it isn't necessary to have central airconditioning in a high rise. Window units will serve the purpose. But if you're in hotter Waikiki with its high humidity, you'd want central airconditioning, if possible.

Call Hawaiian Electric Co., ph. 548-7311 at least one week in advance. There's a $15.00 charge for new accounts. A deposit of $100 may be waived with a letter from your previous electric company provider.

Gas - call BHP Gas Co., ph. 526-0066, at least one business day in advance. Security deposit of $75.00 may be waived with a letter of good credit from your previous provider.

Water bills are moderate. Call Board of Water Supply, 527-6184 at least one business day in advance. No deposit. Sewage charges are included.

Telephone service is provided by GTE Hawaiian Telephone Co., and you have a choice of four long distance carriers. Cable TV service is available in most areas. Call Oceanic Cable, 625-8100, at least two weeks in advance. Standard installation costs under $40.00. You won't be able to receive programs in a high rise building without cable. Rabbit ears won't work.

Over all, utilities are quite reasonable. Not having to heat or aircondition your home or condo is a real benefit. If you're living in a cool area, you won't need more than a ceiling or portable fan.

CLOTHING

This factor in living costs can compensate for higher food and gasoline. You'll certainly not need heavy winter clothing. One sweater or light jacket for our cold 65 degree days. Lots of cotton and silk. Local dressing is extremely casual. Men wear cotton aloha shirts everywhere, and you seldom see a coat and tie. Women wear loose fitting muumuus, jeans, shorts and a tee shirt. Rubber thong slippers are worn practically everywhere. Your clothing budget can be extremely low depending on your attitude. Try shopping at the Swap Meet at Aloha Stadium on Wednesdays, Saturdays, and Sundays. You'll be astonished at the bargains. This is where the locals shop for clothes and many other items.

TRANSPORTATION: YOUR CAR OR THE BUS?

Operating a car on Oahu is expensive. Gasoline is about $1.90 per gallon. Parking fees in downtown Honolulu are expensive. On the other hand, you're not driving long distances as you do on the mainland.

I wouldn't advise a newcomer to try to drive on Oahu until you really become familiar with place names and feel comfortable behind the wheel. Traffic is frustrating. The Hawaiian street names will give you pause. In other words, you'll say "Huh? What's that?"

Start out with The Bus. Honolulu has terrific bus service. Fast, frequent, and cheap. You can buy a bus pass for $15.00 per month. Unlimited mileage. No parking fees, either. This method of transportation might be so convenient and inexpensive you might want to try it for awhile, and rent a car when you feel you really need one.

LIVING ON $1,600 PER MONTH

Since the biggest dent in your budget is housing, you'd need to relocate where housing costs are low to keep within this budget. Rents today are reasonable and choices plentiful.

Obviously, renting a house on Oahu is costly with the median cost of a home at $330,000. A condominium is your best bet. The average cost of a one bedroom condo is $800.00.

Therefore, your monthly budget for two adults might look like this:

MONTHLY BUDGET

Rent	$800
Food	$450
Power Bill	$70
Telephone	$58
The Bus	$30
Water	$20
Misc. (barber, videos)	$77
Cable TV	$33
Total	**$1,538**

You won't have any difficulty spending more. Presents, medical and dental bills not covered by insurance, and unforeseen emergencies will crop up. However, two can live as cheaply here as in many large mainland cities.

Happily, much of the entertainment in Hawaii is outdoors and is free - swimming, surfing, fishing, and frequent outdoor concerts and shows. For example, try the Kapiolani Bandstand at Kapiolani Park on Sunday afternoons at 2:00 p.m. There's usually a free concert and some excellent hula dancing. On Friday at noon, there are frequent concerts at Iolani Palace, where you can brown bag it, sit on the lawn and enjoy the music! Also, stroll along the fence at Waikiki Zoo on Wednesdays, Saturdays, and Sundays, and look at the art exhibitions.

To be sure, there's not room for savings or investments on this budget. It's a bare bones budget. But if you're frugal, paradoxically you can live the life of a millionaire enjoying a perfect climate, beautiful surroundings, exquisite ocean views, and a healthy outdoors lifestyle. Remember, **Hawaii residents happen to live longer than their counterparts in the other 49**

states! The pure fresh air, clean water, and generally pollution free environment is remarkably healthful.

Think of it. You're surrounded by ocean for thousands of miles, so all of that acid rain, nuclear ooze, and carbon monoxide will be dissipated before it reaches our shores. We have our own carbon monoxide, of course, but the trade winds do a good job of blowing the discharge out to sea. There are good reasons to smile every day when you wake up to sunshine, blue skies, and a shining blue sea just waiting for you to jump in for a morning swim. At the Portland Airport, a skycap told me that he could always spot the people from Hawaii "because they're always smiling and laughing!" I answered: "That's true - because they're on their way home!"

MEDICAL FACILITIES

Of the State's over 5,000 licensed physicians, ninety percent are on Oahu. This concentration of doctors creates a situation wherein most of the specialists are there. This makes it difficult for outer island patients, and some specialists visit the neighbor islands once or twice a month to see patients there.

You have the advantage of the best medical care in the State, and best hospitals, if you live on Oahu.

Likewise dental care on the island is excellent. There are more than enough dentists to service the population, and dental specialists such as surgeons and orthodontists are located in Honolulu.

For those needing long-term nursing care, there is at the present time a real shortage of long term care beds in nursing homes. The private sector is attempting to fill the gap and small care homes are applying for variances to operate in residential communities.

ECONOMIC BRIGHT SPOTS: TOURISM AND THE RECENT RETAIL REVOLUTION

TOURISM

Tourism exploded after World War II with the advent of commercial aviation. Gains in tourism since 1945 have been mind-boggling. It has replaced agricultural and Federal defense spending, which used to dominate the Hawaiian economy.

Today, except for Las Vegas, Hawaii is the fastest growing vacation destination, and tourism generates more than $9 billion per year. In fact, total revenues generated by tourism account for over one-third of Hawaii's gross domestic product, more than any other state in the nation.

Because of its unique geographical location as the Crossroads of the Pacific, Hawaii looks forward to increasing numers of visitors from the Orient - fom Japan, Korea, Malaysia, and eventually from China.

THE RECENT RETAIL REVOLUTION

The area stretching from Waikiki to the Dole Cannery outlets past downtown Iwilei is fast becoming one of the world's largest and best shopping destinations for Asian tourists, attacting an affluent shop till you drop crowd. Numerous Asian visitors ae coming to Hawaii for the primary purpose of shopping. Many Japanese tourists arrive in Honolulu with long shopping lists and targeted stores.

With expansions planned in Waikiki, Ala Moana, Ward Warehouse, Dole Cannery, Aloha Tower, and Waikele, it's nothing short of a retail revolution in the making. Considering the sheer numbers of people in Asia along with the economic potential, Hawaii is poised to reap tremendous growth in retailing.

Japan is the focus now, but it's paving the way for an influx of Korean, Taiwanese, and Singaporean, and Malaysian shoppers. And China is next in line. Because of its sheer size,

China may evolve into the greatest consumer market the world has ever seen.

Right now, there are hundreds of mainland retailers wanting in on the action, for they're learned that Hawaii stores are top grossing establishments. They see that Asian visitors have become moreWesternized and want American products. This retail revolution portends a real growth opportunity for Hawaii's future.

SCHOOLS

Oahu offers sunshine, surfing, Mai Tais and radiant sunsets, but it also offers a sense of history, many cultures, and a strong emphasis on education.

Hawaii's best private high schools are Punahou Academy, which is rated among the top ten best prep schools in the nation, Iolani (both on Oahu), and Hawaii Preparatory Academy in Waimea on the Big Island.

These schools are very expensive and not easy to gain admission. Your child has to be an excellent student and needs super references. There are many more applicants than place openings in spite of their expensive tuition. But if you want your child to attend an Ivy League college upon graduation, these schools will give him/her the background. Punahou is heavily endowed, and their computer system is remarkable for a high school. Most graduating students have already taken college level courses.

The University of Hawaii at Manoa is also excellent, and is considered to be a major international university with many students from the Pacific Rim, the mainland, and over sixty foreign countries. UH Manoa operates satellite systems on the neighbor islands with five community college two year programs, and three four year programs offered in Hilo (Hawaii), Manoa (Oahu), and a Leeward Oahu campus. Tuition at UH was very reasonable until 1996 when tuition was given a hefty raise.

Chaminade University in Honolulu is a fine private school, as is Brigham Young University at Laie on Windward Oahu. There's another private institution of higher learning on Oahu -

Hawaii Pacific Unitersity in downtown Honolulu and its Windward campus.

Elementary and high schools have a spotty reputation for teaching basic math, English, history, and science to Hawaii's students. SAT scores have been dismal, ranking with states in the Deep South. Ask to see the school's SAT scores before you commit.

Hawaii has many dedicated teachers and administrators who have been trying for years to improve the situation, and many improvements have been made. Still, in the public school system, some schools stand out as being much better than others. You need to talk to parents in the community who can clue you in as to which schools seem to do a better job. In Hawaii, 22% of students attend private schools, because parents believe that their children won't get a satisfactory education in public schools.

Hawaii has a large Asian population. Traditionally Asian parents put a premium on education and inspire their children to work hard in school. Asian students stand out as scholars in universities across the mainland.

You'll find Honolulu to be a sophisticated, cosmopolitan city, with many very well educated residents. If you compare the Honolulu Star Bulletin newspaper, for example, with others on the mainland such as the Las Vegas Review Journal or the Pensacola News, you'll be surprised at its superior journalistic quality and English language skills.

RECREATION AND CULTURAL FACILITIES

IOLANI PALACE

King & Richards St., downtown next to the State Capitol Building. This is America's only royal palace, interesting to visit. The Royal Hawaiian band plays a free concert at noon every Friday. Pack up a picnic lunch, sit on the grass, and enjoy the music.

BISHOP MUSEUM

1525 Bernice Street. Contains artifacts and collections from Hawaii and the South Seas that you won't see elsewhere. Information: 847-3511

ARIZONA MEMORIAL

Pearl Harbor. More recent history comes to life where the Memorial stands above the sunken battleship which still holds the remains of hundreds of sailors entombed duing the Japanese attack on Pearl Harbor on December 7, 1941. Information for directions: 423-1341

CHINATOWN

Take a walking tour downtown and gain insight into Honolulu's colorful Chinese heritage.

UNIVERSITY OF HAWAII AT MANOA

A beautiful campus to visit. The East-West Center is noted for academic intechange among U.S., Asian, and Pacific scholars. Best libraries on the island.

POLYNESIAN CULTURAL CENTER

55-370 Kamehameha Hwy., Laie. This popular cluster of villages is located on the Windward side of the island about an hour's drive from Waikiki. Don't miss their Polynesian dancing shows. Seven recreated Polynesian villages. Information: 293-3333 or 923-1861, 1-800-347-7060. Between $16 and $30 per person.

WAOLI TEA ROOM

3016 Oahu Ave. Ph. 988-2131. Deep in Manoa Valley. Call for directions and reservations. Lunch only. This is still old Hawaii at its best.

SEA LIFE PARK

Makapuu Point. Exceptional whale and dolphin shows. Home to the only wholphins in the world. Yes, they're a cross between a whale and a dolphin. Very entertaining. Ph. 259-7933 for hours and price of admission.

PALI LOOKOUT

Take Hwy. 61 from Honolulu through Nuuanu Valley and you'll climb to the lookout point at the top of the pali (cliff). This affords a fantastic view of the Windward side of the island. It's also a historic site where King Kamehameha's warriors fought a ferocious battle and defeated Oahu's ruler by pushing his army over the cliff in 1795.

WAIKIKI AQUARIUM

2777 Kalakaua Ave., Ph. 923-9741. Fabulous little aquarium containing over 300 marine species. Admission is only $2.50 and well worth it.

This list is by no means exhaustive. There are so many places to go and attractions to see that you'll have many delightful adventures covering the territory. More fun places to visit:

The **Hawaii Maritime Museum** with its schooner **Falls of Clyde** located downtown at Pier 7 near the Aloha Tower, the **Aloha Tower Marketplace,** the **International Marketplace** in Waikiki, and the **Honolulu Academy of Arts,** 900 S. Beretania St., Ph. 532-8700.

FREEBIES FOR THE FAMILY

Manoa Falls Trail - a lovely pool for a cool dip at the end of the trail.

Discovery Zone at Waikele Center. Information 671-5347. Indoor play centers for children.

Jungle River - miniature golf. Ph. 488-8808. Not a freebie, but inexpensive entertainment.

The Bus - around the island for $1.00. Pack a picnic lunch.
Ilikai Hotel - ride the outdoor glass elevator. What a view!

Kakaako Waterfront Park - slides for the kids.

TIP: Hawaii drivers tend to be more courteous than those found elsewhere. So if you don't drive aggressively, and are patient, you'll find that others will wave and defer to you. What a pleasant surprise! Hawaii, with its strong Oriental community, places a great value on being polite, not loud and rude. If you

128

want to make friends with local people, they prize patience, modesty, and politeness. Don't forget to remove your shoes when you enter a home as a guest!

CHAPTER 6. JOB OPPORTUNITIES

Most of the job opportunities in the Hawaiian Islands are to be found on Oahu where there are a wide variety of jobs available in many categories and many industries except manufacturing. The unempoyment rate on Oahu in 2000 is hovering around 5%. Unemployment on the neighbor islands is much higher, particularly since many jobs have recently been lost in sugar and pineapple.

Job opportunities are scarce on the neighbor islands, and unless you are a professional (doctor, lawyer, accountant, dentist, schoolteacher, nurse, realtor, banker), the vast majority of jobs are in tourism or service jobs which pay minimum wage. You do better if you can collect tips in addition. Young men and women usually end up looking for work on Oahu. A few may work on Oahu during the week and fly home on weekends. Some have started their own small retail or service businesses.

The major employers in Hawaii are: The State of Hawaii, Cities and Counties, Military, the Tourist Industry (Hotels, Airlines, Restaurants), Medical Centers, Schools, Banks, Shipping and Moving Companies, Retail Stores, Insurance Companies, Realty Companies, Utility and Telephone Companies, Automobile Dealerships and Service Stations.

CAN I FIND A JOB EASILY?

That depends on whether your skills are in demand. We've known of a newcomer from Atlanta that landed with $150 in his pocket - all he had in the world - that found housing and a well-paid job immediately through the classified section of the newspaper. (He found shared accommodations where his roomate was willing to wait for his first paycheck). On the other hand, there have been others who took sixty to ninety days to find employment and who have had to work at two or three jobs to make ends meet.

You stand a better chance for rapid employment if you are a well trained, degreed professional (doctor, dentist, nurse, computer expert, accountant). Good auto mechanics are always in demand. So are dental assistants, computer literate people, good salespeople. Teachers are in short supply. If you speak Japanese you'll be very much in demand for an assortment of jobs from flight attendant to tourism and sales.

The State economy has not yet recovered from the recent recession. It is very much tied in with the California economy. Usually when California recovers, Hawaii's economy perks up about ten months later. Although tourism is again on the increase, real estate sales are slow, and construction has been anemic in the nineties. Construction of the new, multi-million dollar convention center in Waikiki may spark a construction comeback. The State of Hawaii and the Cities and Counties have had a hiring freeze in the nineties. Military bases, including Pearl Harbor, have been downsizing.

A note of caution: To make it here you need to be very flexible and open-minded. You may have to accept a job that you haven't trained for, or that pays less than you are used to earning. You may need to start your own little business in addition to working for someone else. Our economy is based on tourism and hospitality.

WAGES

Wages on Oahu, in spite of the high cost of living, have historically lagged behind those paid in San Francisco or Los Angeles. Some examples follow:

Secretary - $1,600 to $2,000 monthly.
Legal Secretary - $2,500 to $3,000
Waiter - $1,600 to $2,000, including tips, at a medium priced restaurant.
Skilled waiter - $2,500 to $3,000 at an upscale restaurant
Auto mechanic - $35,000 to $40,000 per year
Insurance Agent - rookie $30,000 per year rising to $100,000 after seven years if successful
Teacher - $25,000 per year rising to $36,000 after ten years
Dentist - $117,000 per year

Accountant - $36,000 to $75,000 depending on credentials and experience

Medical Doctor - $75,000 to $200,000 per year

Sales agent - Mostly hourly paid jobs. If you speak Japanese, you'll earn a premium. It's possible, for example, to earn $3,000 per month working as a sales clerk in an upscale dress or wedding shop. Japanese corporation employers usually pay excellent wages and benefits.

Note that the white collar professional jobs normally pay less than on the mainland, as much as thirty-five percent less. Consider that plus the increased costs for housing and you have a brain drain - Hawaii's brightest young people moving to the mainland. During this recession, Hawaii's job count declined by 2.3 percent, compared to an increase of 11.8 percent on the mainland. Jobs are really tight, particularly on the outer islands.

At local libraries you can find statistics from the Hawaii Dept. of Labor and Industrial Relations which give average wages for typical occupations, and projections of those occupations which are expected to grow until 2005. These include all of the assistants to the medical and legal professions, those in the travel and hotel industries, and all of the service jobs that keep the tourist industry humming. See Appendix B for a detailed list of major employers on each island. You can also access the Hawaii State Data Book via the internet at http://www.hawaii.gov/dbedt/index.html

GROUND TRANSPORTATION

Bus service is really excellent in the city of Honolulu. The fare is $1.00. Buses run frequently, and since parking downtown is expensive, you may prefer to bus to work instead of fighting traffic jams. Although some bicycle and ride mopeds, this is really not advisable from a safety standpoint.

HOW DO I GO ABOUT FINDING A JOB?

We recommend that you start making contacts while you are still on the mainland. First, attempt to use direct mail to tap the "hidden job market" before you try the employment agencies.

This means that you attempt to do direct mailing to a small target market of employers. Choose the industries you're interested in, get the names of companies in it and their executives, and do a direct mailing of your resume to as many prospective target employers as you can - a minimum of 25 to a maximum of 50. You should average a response rate of three to ten percent, and this method very often leads to jobs.

Start sending out resumes while you are still on the mainland. Most employers will be willing to do preliminary interviews with you over the telephone once they have received your resume, and it's possible to secure employment even before you arrive, providing you are skilled in some way, have a stable work history, and/or there is a shortage of local applicants for the job.

I can't emphasize enough the importance of good references. If you have any contacts at all in Hawaii, use networking because a local reference is worth its weight in gold.

Subscribe to the local newspaper at least two months before you move. Study the Classified Ads for job opportunities so that you become familiar with jobs that are advertised before your arrival.

Newspapers:

Oahu - (808) 538-6397
Maui - (808) 521-4653
Kauai - (808)245-3681
Hawaii -
Hilo (808) 935-6621
Kona (808) 329-9311

WHERE CAN I CALL FOR JOB LISTINGS?

The following is a list of employers to call for job listings currently available: The local telephone area code is (808).

Jobs On Oahu	541-2791
Veterans Employment	586-8828
Sheraton Hotels	931-8294
Outrigger Hotels	921-6955
State of Hawai	587-0977
Wahiawa Hospita	621-4401
Straub Clinic	948-0606
Clerical	948-0507
Managerial	948-0505
Hyatt Hotels Jobs	923-1234
City of Honolulu	523-4303
First Hawaiian Bank	525-5627
Employment Training	541-2518
Civilian Employment	438-9301
Bank of Hawaii	537-8688
Bank of America	545-6463

When you call, be sure to ask for not only the address, but the name of the person to whom you should direct your resume.

TEMPORARY AGENCIES

This is a fast way to get your foot in the door, and it very often leads to a permanent job:

Labor Services	591-4950
Kokua Nurses	594-2326
Kelly	536-9346
Interim	942-2233
Dunhill	524-1733
Career Connections	537-4848
Altres	373-1955
Adia	533-8889

Account Temps	531-8056
Western	524-0411
Temp Help Services	832-0050
Staff, Inc.	521-8941
Snelling	524-0100
Select	483-0005
Sales Consultants	521-7828
Remedy	949-3669
Nurse Finders	522-6050
Norrell	531-9700
Manpower	922-3166

EMPLOYMENT AGENCIES

Since these agencies commonly charge 60% to 65% of your first month's pay, obviously it would be great if you could find a job on your own. However, some of these agencies do a real service in matching people to positions:

Island Network	944-5544
Job City, Inc.	942-2000
Lam Associates	947-9815
A-1 Employment	947-1205
Triple Services	955-7355
Strictly Professional	533-8313
Sheer Careers	833-3182
Assoc. Employment	537-3381
Beneficial Employer	526-4121
Dana's Housekeeping	732-9490
Employee Leasing Co.	591-4490
Executive Recruiters	521-5991
Hawaii Nannies	521-6262

CRUISE SHIP JOBS

If you don't get sea-sick easily, you might look ino one of the cruise ship jobs with the S.S. Independence or Constitution. These ships ply between the islands and frequently advertise for shipboard help. Jobs include room and board and pay well. Phone 808-847-3172.

UNION JOBS

State Teachers Ass'n	833-2711
Firefighters	949-1566
Plumbers	536-5454
Electrical Workers	847-5341
Carpenters Union	847-5761

JOB BENEFITS

Hawaii law requires employers to provide full medical coverage for employees who work more than twenty hours per week. Coverage is excellent. Some of Hawaii's employers try to avoid this expense by offering part-time jobs. Hawaii also has Workers Compensation insurance coverage for workers injured on the job. Hawaii has been progressive in providing legislated liberal benefits for its workers.

If you are persistent, and have marketable skills, you'll be successful in your search. We welcome you to our beautiful islands and our tradition of hospitality, but because jobs are in short supply we frequently favor hiring local residents over newcomers unless the newcomer is better qualified.

CHAPTER 7. THE MECHANICS OF MOVING

MOVING COSTS

The least expensive way to ship household furniture and boxes is to hire experienced packers yourself, and then rent a container to be delivered to your home from one of the ocean cargo companies. Be sure your packers know how to pack a container for overseas shipment. Furniture has to be well padded and packed tightly so it won't roll around on the ocean.

Matson Navigation Co. and Sea-Land Service Co. service Honolulu regularly. On the West Coast, Matson is the oldest, biggest, and to my mind most experienced. Four Matson ships arrive in Honoluu Harbor each week - two from Los Angeles, and two from Oakland (one of which originates in Seattle).

Call them at their San Francisco office: 1-800-462-8766. They ship from Long Beach, Oakland, and Portland/Seattle. Their fees are approximately $1,900 for a twenty foot container, and $3,325 for a forty foot container. Yes, you can share a container.

These fees do not include transport from the docks in Hawaii to your home address, which could cost an additional trucking fee of $100 to $500, depending on location.

From the East Coast, call John Steere Co. at 215-922-6610. Ask to speak to John Ross and he will advise you and work up a written estimate. A 20 foot container shipped from a Florida dock costs about a whopping $4,000 which doesn't include packing and insurance. If your goods are shipped to one of the outer islands, your bill for a twenty foot container including packing and insurance could total $6,700. Wow! Really not cost effective. From the East Coast your goods would be shipped through the Panama Canal.

Since the vessel is ocean bound and you may be shipping through rough waters, your household goods need to be tightly packed. The best way to ship breakables is inside a round, heavy cardboard container with a metal banded top seal which you can purchase from moving companies. This container works much better than cardboard boxes, and it's rare to find a broken article when you unpack. Your insurance may not cover crystal, china, and glass breakables, and may be limited to $250 recovery for any box **you** pack.

Unless you have furniture that is dear to your heart, antiques, or other items that you can't bear to give up, it's not cost effective to ship furniture. You can start fresh in Hawaii. Also, consider that anything chrome or metal will need special coating to resist corrosion from salt air here in Hawaii.

People are always arriving and leaving and you can pick up great quality items at garage sales if you don't want to pay retail prices.

Ship your books at the book rate of $1.24 per pound through the post office. You can mail other boxes through the post office for $.57 per pound surface mail. It'll take four to six weeks to get here, but it's one third the price that moving companies charge.

Probably you'd be better off selling most of your furniture, because the climate is different here. Lighter pastel colors and fabrics work best here for clothes and furnishings. Your woolen clothes would need special protection here from our happy Hawaiian silver fish. Popular furnishings here tend to be lightweight rattan, lots of cotton fabric, and glass topped tables.

Caveat: Even though the moving companies advertise "a quality move", and even though they tout "experienced packers", frequently shipments arrive with scarred and nicked furniture, broken legs, some theft, and a real hassle collecting from insurance companies. Be present when the seal is broken on your container. If it's already broken, there may be theft or damage.

CARS

What should you do with your car? Ship it? By all means, if you can afford to do so. While it doesn't pay to ship your car from Honolulu to the mainland, it certainly does pay to ship it here, as cars are more expensive here. Matson's shipping rates are about $850.00 one way depending on size. Young Brothers, who ship cars on barges between the islands, has recently applied for an 8% rate hike, which, if granted, will increase the cost of outer island delivery.

You'd probably want to drive your car and ship it from one of the West Coast ports. Delivery service is available from points East, but it greatly adds to the cost of shipping.

If you opt for shipping from, for example, Long Beach, call Matson in advance and they'll discuss shipping schedules with you and send you a map to find them. It'll take about 21 days for your car to arrive in Honolulu. You'd have to book a reaservation, then drive to Terminal Island in Long Beach. The whole procedure is quite simple and they give excellent directions and instructions.

When you arrive at the dock, your car should have about a quarter tank of gas in it. Years ago you could ship items in your car. Now, because of rampant theft on the docks, it has to be shipped empty.

If you don't want to go through the hassle of shipping your car, sell your car on the mainland and buy one here. You can pick up an inexpensive, older Nissan or Toyota. You'll want a smaller car in Hawaii. Easy to park, and since gasoline prices are so high, you'll want to get good mileage. That's a reliable Honda or Toyota which are in great demand here. You won't be driving long distances as on the mainland, so you don't need a big, heavy car with the long wheel base for comfort.

If you do ship your car here, and decide to return to the mainland in a couple of years, it's not unusual for you to be able to sell it here for what you paid for it on the mainland. Put up a Car For Sale sign up at bulletin boards at the military bases. Those young men are frequently buying and selling cars, the love of their lives at that young age.

Once your car has arrived, you'll have ten days to register it with the County Dept. of Motor Vehicles for your temporary permit. Try to get your Hawaii's driver's license as soon as possible for it will entitle you to breaks on rental cars and other "kamaaina" discounts on hotels and inter-island airfares.

141

TIP: Get a guaranteed delivery date for your car. Ask the Matson agent. If it's late, the moving company may reimburse you for a rental car or other expenses.

Expect that your car battery will be dead upon delivery.

Also note that when you drive your car to a beach on Oahu, do not leave any valuables in the car, not even in a locked trunk while you go merrily off hiking or swimming. Thieves have been known to break in, remove the back seat and get into the trunk.

PETS

One of the hardest thing a pet owner who ships his pet to Hawaii has to do is put his cat or dog in quarantine. Hawaii has no rabies and wants to keep it that way. Rabies would be a horrible problem here, for it would be spread rapidly by the resident mongoose population.

Only animals from rabies free countries of New Zealand and Australia escape incarceration ." The "prison term" is now 30 days. The cost is substantial and varies as to whether the pet is a dog or cat - around $500 - $1,000 per pet. Write to the State Quarantine Animal Shelter at 99-770 Moanalua Road, Aiea, Hi. 96721 for a brochure, or phone 808-483-7171. Fax 808.483-7161.

The pre-qualification requirements include two rabies vaccinations, not less than 60 days apart, and a health certificate as well as a microchip implant and rabies blood test. You're looking at about $200 in pre-qualification expenses.

CHAPTER 8. THE PRICE OF PARADISE

Are these islands really a Paradise? Remember that Paradise is in the eye of the beholder - a matter of perception. If you're unhappy in Detroit, you bring yourself with you and you'll find lots of things about Hawaii to criticize. But, to paraphrase Frank Sinatra's rendition of "New York, New York", if you can't make it here (be happy) you can't be happy anwhere!

Many former islanders who have left for greener financial opportunities would be back in a flash if they could. On Oahu today, the cost of living is a whopping 35% higher than in the average mainland city, as compiled by the Bank of Hawaii. The cost of buying and renting is skyhigh for people moving East to West, but looks like a bargain for those moving from West (such as Tokyo or Singapore) to East.

The drop in housing rentals on Oahu has provided a window of opportunity for those wanting to try island living. Food costs are higher than on the mainland, but you can cut this down by smart shopping as we've discussed in this book. Utility costs are higher per kilowatt hour, but we don't need to heat our homes and seldom need airconditioning. We don't need winter clothes, either. Overall, the islands are a retiree's dream. Those of you that are younger need to do some fancy footwork to line up a job or business opportunity before you decide to make the move.

Hawaii's beauty is legendary. The climate is mild, the residents are pleasant and friendly, and the environment is a happy one. People actually smile at you without wanting something, and are courteous. Drivers stop for pedestrians as they cross the street. People seem to be enjoying life.

If you like water sports such as swimming, surfing, windsurfing, or fishing, it's the greatest. That's not to say that it's a perfect paradise. Paradise, after all, is made up of people. Are you perfect? But you'll hear a lot of people say that they wouldn't leave here for love or money, and that they're just so glad to get back when they step off that airplane, feel the balmy air, see the clouds scudding over the Koolaus, and realize they're home.

APPENDIX A
PRONUNCIATION GUIDE

Most visitors speaking their native language, whether Japanese, French, German, or that most difficult of languages, English, have experienced the difficulty of attempting to learn another language, and are frightened at what appears to be a strange and difficult tongue; strange, perhaps, but definitely **not difficult!**

Perhaps some simple rules will help. After all, the Hawaiian alphabet contains only 12 letters, the 5 vowels and 7 consonants, and the 5 vowels are all pronounced (no silent letters), and always pronounced the same way! Now, how difficult could that be?

Let's take the vowels first, (pronounced as in Spanish) in alphabetical order:

A, pronounced "ah"--(like the dentist orders, "say ah", or the 'a' in father). Example: "Aloha" - pronounced: Ah-low'-hah, with the accent on the second sylable, not the third!

E, pronounced like the `American' a, as in fate. Example:"Pueo" (owl)--pronounced poo-a'-oh.

I, pronounced like the `American' e, as in "see". Example: "Hilo" (a small town on the Big Island of Hawaii)--pronounced: Hee"low.

O, pronounced like the `American' o, as in "low". Example: "Okole" (part of the anatomy colloquially referred to as "buns") pronounced: Oh-ko'lay.

U, pronounced like the double o in "too" (not as "you".) Example: "Puka"--pronounced: Poo-ka.

There are only seven consonants in the Hawaiian alphabet, pronounced basically as in English, except for the "w", which in pure Hawaiian (which doesn't exist anymore, except possibly as spoken by Hawaiians living on the island of Niihau, a privately owned island) is pronounced as a "v". Currently, the "w" is pronounced as a "v" in words like "Hawaii", "Waikiki", "Hawi", and "Kaaawa".

Did the triple "a" vowel in Kaaawa give you pause? Remember, **all** of the vowels are pronounced. Kaaawa is pronounced: "Ka-ah-ah-va". Simple, no? (Kaaawa is a little town on the Windward side of Oahu).

One other rule: the accent on Hawaiian words is almost always on the next to last syllable. Exceptions include "Hawi", pronounced "Ha-wi'", not "Ha'-wi". (A small town in Kohala on the Big Island).

This isn't an exhaustive study of the Hawaiian language, but it will help. At least you won't be pronouncing the 50th State's name as "High-wah-yah", as I've heard it said in the Mid-West, and which makes local people wince. They also wince when they hear Wah-ki'-ki, instead of Wai-ki-ki'.

Worthwhile, too, is getting to know a few of the commonly used pidgin expressions and Hawaiian words that have been adopted by the "kamaainas" (long time residents) even when speaking English

The "aina" in "kamaaina" means land, literally guardian of the land. The Hawaiians regarded themselves as environmentally friendly custodians of the land long before it became fashionable to do so.

Local language is often peppered with common Hawaiian words, plus Japanese, Chinese, and Filipino common words. That's why I said you could understand the language - well, almost. If a person lapsed into the local pidgin English (a mixture of all these words) you'd find it unintelligible. Superfluous words are left out. "Where are you going" becomes "Whea you go, huh?". You almost have to grow up with it to make any sense out of it. It has a peculiar singsong sound to it, also. Takes a little getting used to.

COMMON HAWAIIAN WORDS AND SLANG PHRASES

Aloha - hello, goodbye, love
Aloha nui loa - love to you

Aloha kakou (a toast) - love to the world

Assa malla you? - What's the matter with you

Auwe (pronounced Au-way) - my goodness, good grief, how awful

Hana hou - one more time, do it again once more

Haole - Caucasian, white man or woman

Hapa-haole - half-white

Hui - group of investors or social club

Imu - hole in the ground lined with hot coals to roast a pig

Kai- water, the ocean or sea

Kala (pronounced ka-la') - money

Kamaaina - long time resident of Hawaii as opposed to malihini (newcomer)

Kanaka - Hawaiian

Kane - man, men, appears on rest room doors

Kapakahi - all fouled up, not straight

Kapu - keep out, forbidden

Kokua - help, as in "I ask for your kokua."

Lua - toilet, "Where's the lua?"

Luau - barbecue party where pig is smoked in an imu

Mahalo - thank you (seen on trash barrels)

Mahu - gay, homosexual

Makai - towards the sea

Mauka - towards the mountain (Makai and Mauka are often used in giving directions).

Mauna Kea - white mountain. (On the Big Island - it's covered with snow in the winter).

Mauna Loa - long mountain. On the Big Island.

Muumuu - long, loose-fitting dress worn day or night anywhere, introduced by missionairies

Nui - big as in opu nui (big stomach)

Ohana - family

Okole - butt, as in "Move your okole", meaning "Hurry up."

Ono - delicious

Pakalolo - Maui wowee, marijuana

Pake - prounounced Pah'-kay - Chinese

Pau - done, finished, "Are you pau?" Pau hana - finished with work at the end of the day

Popolo - black person, Negro
Puka - hole, as in the "The Dutch boy put his finger in the puka in the dam to stop the water." Pupus - bite sized delicacies, hors d'oeuvres
Wahine - wife, woman, as in "My wahine."
(Seen on restroom doors).
Wikiwiki - hurry, quickly - as in "Wikiwiki Bus".

Every language has words that are particularly apt in expressing the **exact** meaning of something that defies translation into another language; such as "Savoir faire" in French, or "Gemulichkeit" in German. So it is with the Hawaiian language. What better "all purpose" words could rival "puka" (hole), or "kapakahi" (crooked), for example?

Pidgin directions, too, are frequently adopted. The story is told about the mainland haole (white mainlander) trying to find his way with a map in the maze of frequently unmarked streets in Honolulu, Trying to orient his map, he asked a local resident,
"Please, sir, which way is North?"
To which the amiable fellow replied:

"Assa malla you? (What's the matter with you?) We got Mauka and Makai, we got Diamond Head and Ewa, we no got North!" (Mauka - toward the mountains, Makai - toward the ocean, Diamond Head - toward the South, Ewa - toward the North).

With that bit of scholarly advice, we bid a fond "Aloha!"

APPENDIX B

MAJOR EMPLOYERS

GOVERNMENT JOBS - ALL ISLANDS

Federal jobs

Federal Employment Information Center
U. S. Office of Personnel Management
300 Ala Moana #5316
Honolulu, Hi.96813
541-2791
Neighbor isles call 541-2784

State Dept. of Human Resources Development
235 S. Beretania St. #1100
Honolulu, Hi. 96813
Phone 587-0977
Neighbor Isles phone 1-800-468-4644 x70977

Judiciary
417 S. King St.
Honolulu, Hi. 96813
539-4949

Dept. of Education
1390 Miller St.
Honolulu, Hi. 9968133
586–3420 - teacher hiring
586-3422 other jobs
Honolulu City & County
Department of Personnel
550 S. King St.
Honolulu, Hi. 96813
523-4301

Hawaii County
Department of Civil Service
101 Aupuni St. #133
Hilo, Hi. 96720
961-8361

Maui County
Department of Personnel Services
200 S. High St.
Wailuku, Hi. 96793
243-7850

Kauai County
Department of Personnel Services
4444 Rice Street
Lihue, Hi. 96766
241-6595

HAWAII

Note that you need to be a Hawaii resident to apply for state government positions. You cannot apply from another state. Call the State of Hawaii 24 hour job line at 808.587-0977.

Hawaii State and County also publishes a newsletters with public notices and jobs available on all of the islands. Call RFD Publications Inc. 808.235-5881. The electronic version is updated every Monday and may be seen at http://www.midweek.com

State of Hawaii
Governor's State Information Office
75-5706 Kuakini, Rm. 112
Kailua, Hi. 96740
329-9066

University of Hawaii at Hilo
200 W. Kawili St.
Hilo, Hi. 96720
974-7311

City & County job hotline 961-8618

Call or write for a detailed list of address and phone numbers. Includes fire department, parks and recreation, housing and community development, liquor control, mayor's office, parks and recreation, police department, public works department, and the water supply department.

FEDERAL GOVERNMENT

The federal government maintains only skeleton crews on the outer islands. The federal job information center's office of personnel management is located on Oahu. The only outer island presence maintained by the federal government is in the national parks, the post offices, and the ubiquitous I.R.S., also the Social Security Administration. The military branches also maintain their central offices on Oahu.

TOURIST INDUSTRY

HOTELS

Naniloa Hotel
93 Banyan Dr.
Hilo, Hi. 96720
969-3333

Hilo Hawaiian Hotel
71 Banyan Dr.
Hilo, Hi. 96720
935-9361

Seaside Hotel
126 Banyan Way
Hilo, Hi. 96720
935-0821

Uncle Billy's
87 Banyan Dr.
Hilo, Hi. 96720
935-0861
Uncle Billy's Kona
329-1393

Volcano House
P. O. Box 53
Hawaii National Park, Hi. 96718
967-7321

Prince Hotel
62-100 Kaunaoa Dr.
Kamuela, Hi. 96743
882-5770

Four Seasons
100 Kaupulehu Dr.
Kaupulehu, Hi. 96740
874-8000

Mauna Lani Bay Hotel
68-1400 Mauna Lani Dr.
Kamuela, Hi. 96743
885-6622

Waikoloa Beach Resort
1020 Keana Pl.
Kamuela, Hi. 96743
886-1000

Outrigger Waikoloan (formerly Royal Waikoloan)
1020 Keana Pl.
Kamuela, Hi. 96743
886-1000

Kona Village
P. O. Box 1299
Kailua-Kona 96745
325-5555

King Kamehameha's Kona Beach Hotel
75-5660 Palani Road
Kailua-Kona, Hi. 96740
329-2911

Kona Surf
78-128 Ehukai St.
Kailua-Kona, Hi. 96740
322-3411

HARDWARE STORES

Ace Hardware
74-5500 Kaiwi
Kailua-Kona, Hi. 96740
329-2981
In Keauhou
322-3336
In Capt. Cook
323-2655
In Hilo
660 Kilauea Ave.
961-3741
Kamuela
885-6059
Keeau
966-7170

HPM Hardware and Building Supply
380 Kanoelehua St.
Hilo, Hi. 96720
935-0875

In Kona
329-1634
In Kamuela
885-6036

SECURITY GUARDS

Burns Security Services
1266 Kamehameha Ave.
Hilo, Hi. 96720
969-9288
In Kona
75-5275 Alii Dr.
Kailua-Kona, Hi. 96740
329.4650

Wackenhut of Hawaii
74-5467 Kaiwi St., Unit 4C
Kailua-Kona, Hi. 96740
In Hilo
17 Makaala St., Ste. 101
Hilo, Hi. 96720
935-7463

UTILITIES

Hawaii Electric Light Co.
1200 Kilauea Ave.
Hilo, Hi. 96720
935-1171

GTE Hawaiian Telephone Co.
161 Kinoole St.
Hilo, Hi. 96720
933-6514

Sun Cablevision
74-5605 Luhia St.
Kailua-Kona, Hi. 96740
329-2418

DRUG AND DEPARTMENT STORES

Long's Drugstore
111 E. Puainako St.
Hilo, Hi. 96720
959-5881
In Kona
75-5595 Palani Rd.
329-1380
In Keauhou
78-6831 Alii Drive
Kailua-Kona, Hi. 96740
322-5122

Wal-Mart
75-1015 Henry St.
Kailua-Kona, Hi. 96740
334-0466
In Hilo
325 E. Makaala St.
Hilo, Hi. 96720
967-9115
K-Mart
74-5465 Kamehameha St.
Kailua-Kona, Hi. 96740
326-2331

Sears, Roebuck, & Co.
111 E. Puainako St., Bldg. 2
Hilo, Hi. 96720

Costco
73-5600 Maiau St.
Kailua-Kona 96740
331-4831

Liberty House
Makalapua Center
Kailua-Kona, Hi.
329-6300
In Hilo
Prince Kuhio Plaza
Hilo, Hi. 96720
959-3561

RESTAURANTS

Chart House
75-5770 Alii Dr.
Kailua-Kona 96740
329-2451

Hard Rock Café
75-5801 Alii Dr.
Kailua-Kona 96740
329-8866

Huggo's
75-5828 Kahakai Rd.
Kailua-Kona, 96740
329-1493

Jolly Roger
75-5776 Alii Dr.
Kailua-Kona, 96740
329-1344

Bubba Gump
75-5776 Alii Drive
Kailua-Kona, Hi. 96740
Also on Maui and Oahu
Fax resumes to: 847.518-8331
Attention: Recruitment
www.bubbagump.com

Sizzler
74-5586 Palani Rd.
Kailua-Kona, 96740
329-3374

Denny's
75-1027 Henry St.
Kailua-Kona 96740
334-1313

Bianelli's Pizza
75-240 Nani Kailua Rd.
Kailua-Kona, Hi. 96740
327-1104
Kona Ranch House
75-5653 Ololi St.
Kailua-Kona, Hi. 96740
329-7061

Hukilau Restaurant
421 Kalanikoa
Hilo, Hi. 96720
934-9490

Ken's House of Pancakes
1730 Kamehameha Ave.
Hilo, Hi. 96720
935-8711

There are also fast food restaurants, McDonald's, Wendy's, and Taco Bells island wide, plus many ethnic Italian and Mexican restaurants.

SUPERMARKETS

Safeway
111 E. Puaino St.
Hilo, Hi. 96720
959-5831
In Kona
75-1027 Henry St.
Kailua-Kona, 96740
329-2207

KTA
50 E. Puainako St.
Hilo, Hi. 96720
In Kona
Kona Coast Shopping Center
Kailua-Kona 96740
329-1677
In Keauhou
Box 246
Kailua-Kona, 96745
329–1677

Sack n Save Foods
2100 Kanoelehua Ave.
Hilo, Hi. 96720
959-5831
In Kona
75-5595 Palani Rd.
Kailua-Kona, 96740
326-2729

BOOKSTORES

Border's
75-100 Henry St.
Kailua-Kona 96740
331-1668

Barnes and Noble is on Oahu

BANKS

First Hawaiian Bank
1205 Kilauea Ave.
Hilo, Hi. 96720
933-2260
In Kona
74-5593 Palani Ave.
Kailua-Kona, 96740
329-2461

Bank of Hawaii
120 Pauahi St.
Hilo, Hawaii 96720
In Kona

American Savings Bank
Lanihau Center
Kailua-Kona, Hi. 96740
329-5281
In Hilo
100 Pauahi
Hilo, Hawaii 96720
935-0084

Territorial Savings & Loan
75-5751 Kuakini Hwy. Ste. 107
Kailua-Kona, Hi. 96740

In Hilo
315 Makaala
Hilo, Hawaii 96720
935-3952

HOSPITALS AND CLINICS

Kona Community Hospital
Haukapili St.
Kealakekua, Hi. 96750
322-9311

Hilo Hospital
1190 Waianuenue Ave.
Hilo, Hi. 96720
974-4700

Life Care Center ofHilo
944 W. Kawailani St.
Hilo, Hi. 96720
959-9151

Keauhou Rehabilitation and Health Care Center
78-6957 Kamehameha III Rd.
Kailua-Kona, Hi. 96740
322-2790

Clinical Laboratories of Hawaii
33 Lanihuli
Hilo, Hi. 96720
In Kona
75-170 Hualalai Rd.
Kailua-Kona, 96740
329-2205

North Hawaii Community Hospital
67-1125 Mamalahoa Hwy.
Waimea, Hi. 96738
885-4444

FOOD & LIQUOR WHOLESALERS

Suisan
Box 366
Hilo, Hi. 96721
935-8511

Y. Hata & Co.
300 Kanoelehua Ave.
Hilo, Hi. 96720
935-3321

Paradise Beverages
452 Kalanianaole
Hilo, Hi. 96720
In Kona
73-5881 Olowalu
Kailua-Kona 96740
329-2242

Better Brands
190 Kuawa St.
Hilo, Hi. 96740
935-8664
In Kona
74-5616B Alapa St.
Kailua-Kona, Hi. 96740
326-2768

SCHOOLS

Department of Education
P. O. Box 2360
Honolulu, Hi. 96804
1-800-305-5104
808.586-3420

Frequently there are openings for special education teachers, math and science teachers. The pay scale ranges from approximately $27,000 to $54,000.

University of Hawaii at Hilo
200 W. Kawili St.
Hilo, Hi. 96720
974-7311

Hawaii Community College
200 W. Kawili St.
Hilo, Hi. 96720
974-7311

Hawaii Preparatory Academy
P. O. Box 428
Kamuela, Hi. 96743
885-7321

St. Joseph School
1000 Ululani St.
Hilo, Hi. 96720
935-4936

BUILDING CONTRACTORS

Isemoto Contracting Co., Ltd.
648 Piilani St.
Hilo, Hi. 96720
935-7194
In Kona
74-50398 Kaahumanu Hwy.
Kailua-Kona, Hi. 96740
329-3261

Jas. W. Glover
890 Leilani St.
Hilo, Hi. 96720
935-0871

Kona Operations
Honokohou Harbor
329-4113

Hawaiian Dredging & Construction Co., Ltd.
961-2021

Maryl Construction Co.
75-1000 Henry St.
Ste. 200
Kailua-Kona, Hi. 96740
331-8100

TOUR & TRAVEL AGENTS

Waipio Valley Wagon Tours
P. O. Box 1340
Honokaa, Hi. 96727
775-9518

The Activity Connection
P. O. Box 3380
Kailua-Kona, Hi. 96745
329-1038

Hawaii Forest & Trail, Ltd.
P. O. Box 2975
Kailua-Kona, Hi. 96745
322-8881

Atlantis Submarines Hawaii
329-3175

Capt. Beans Cruises
73-4800 Kanalani St.
Kailua-Kona, Hi. 96745
329-2955

Fair Wind
78-7130 Kaleiopapa St.
Kailua-Kona, Hi. 96740
322-2644

Roberts Hawaii
73-4800 Kanalani St., Ste. 200
Kailua-Kona, Hi. 96740
329-1688
In Hilo
16-188 Melekahiwa
Keaau, Hi. 96749
966-5483

REALTORS

Realty companies provide employment for many Hawaii residents. I haven't included this list because you would first need to become a resident and then pass the sales examination. Local companies prefer that you have a sales license even for working in property rentals. If you're interested, look in the Sunday Classified Section advertisements.

Kona Board of Realtors 808.329-4874
Hilo Board of Realtors 808.935-0827

TIP: Don't overlook timeshare sales, a very lucrative specialty, and one that is growing by leaps and bounds in Hawaii.

MAUI

TOURIST INDUSTRY

HOTELS

Grand Wailea Resort
Human Resources Dept.
3850 Wailea Alanui Drive
Maui, Hi. 96753
Job Hotline 808.874-2400

Four Seasons Resort
3900 Wailea Alanui Drive
Kihei, Hi. 96753
874-8000

Kaanapali Hotel
50 Nohea Kai Dr.
Lahaina, Hi. 96761
667-1400

Hyatt Regency
200 Nohea Kai Dr.
Lahaina, Hi. 96761
661-1234

Embassy Suites
104 Kaanapali Shores Pl.
Lahaina, Hi. 96761
661-2000

Aston Wailea
3700 Wailea Alanui Dr.
Kihei, Hi. 96753
879-1922

Kaanapali Beach Hotel
2525 Kaanapali Pkwy.
Lahaina, Hi. 96761
661-0011

Westin Maui
2365 Kaanapali Pkwy.
Lahaina 96761
667-2525

Kapalua Bay Hotel
1 Bay Dr.
Lahaina, Hi. 96761
669-5656

Maui Marriott Hotel
100 Nohea Kai Dr.
Lahaina, Hi. 96761
667-1200

Maui Prince Hotel
5400 Makena Alanui
Kihei, Hi. 96753
874-1111

Mahana at Kaanapali
110 Kaanapali Shores Pl.
Lahaina, Hi. 96761
661-8751

RESTAURANTS

Makawao Steak House
3612 Baldwin Ave.
Makawao, Hi. 96768
572-8711

Casanova Italian Restaurant & Deli
1188 Makawao Ave.
Makawao, Hi. 96768
572-0220

Mama's Fish House
799 Poho Place
Paia, Maui 96779
579-9248

Longhi's Café
888 Front St.
Lahaina, Hi. 96761
667-7400

Hard Rock Café
900 Front St.
Lahaina, Hi. 96761
667-7400

Denny's Restaurant
840 Wainee St.
Lahaina, Hi. 96761
667-7898
In Kihei
2463 S. Kihei Rd.
Kihei, Hi. 96753
879-0604

International House of Pancakes
70 E. Kaahumanu St.
Kahului, Hi. 96732
871-4000
In Kihei
Azeka Place Shopping Center
Kihei Hi. 96753
879-3445

Chuck's Steak House
Kihei Town Center
Kihei, Hi. 96753
879-0837

Jameson's Grill & Bar
2259 So. Kihei Road
Kihei, Hi. 96753
891-0795

Sam Choy's Kahului Restaurant
275 Kaahumanu Ave.
Kahului, Hi. 96732
893-0366
In Lahaina
900 Front St.
661-3800

Bubba Gump
889 Front St.
Lahaina, Hi. 96761
661-3111

Leilani's
2435 Kaanapali Pkwy.
Lahaina, Hi. 96761
661-4495

Kobe Japanese Steak House
136 Dickenson St.
Llahaina, Hi. 96761
667-5555

Ruth's Chris Steak House
900 Front St.
Lahaina, Hi. 96761
661-8815

The Chart House
1450 Front St.
Lahaina, Hi. 96761
661-0937
In Kahului
500 N. Puunene Ave.
Kahului, Hi. 96732
877-2476
In Kihei
100 Wailea Iki Dr.
Kihei, Hi. 96753
879-2875

Tony Roma's
1819 S. Kihei Rd.
Kihei, Hi. 96753
875-1104

STORES AND DRUGSTORES

Costco
540 Haleakala Hwy.
Kahului, Maui 96732

K Mart
424 Dairy Rd.
Kahului, Hi. 96732

Sears
275 W. Kaahumanu Ave.
Kahului, Hi. 96732
877-2221

Longs Drugstore
Kaahumanu Shopping Center
Kahului, Hi. 96732
877-0041

In Lahaina
1221 Honoapiilani Hwy.
Lahaina, Hi. 96761
667-4384

Liberty House
Kaahumanu Shopping Center
Kahului, Hi. 96732
877-3361

BUILDING CONTRACTORS

Arisumi Brothers, Inc.
291 Dairy Rd.
Kahului, Hi. 96732
877-5014

Fletcher Pacific Construction Co.
172 Alamaha
Kahului, Hi. 96732
877-8725

Hawaiian Dredging Construction Co.
261 Lalo, Ste. A1
Kahului, Hi. 96732
871-0661

Albert C. Kobayashi, Inc.
875 Alua 2nd Floor
Wailuku, Hi. 96793
242-1595

Hygrade Electric Co.
793 Alua St.
Wailuku, Maui 96793
242-1484

BANKS

American Savings Bank
275 Kaahumanu Ave.
Kahului, Hi. 96732
871-5501

Bank of Hawaii
27 Puunene Ave.
Kahului, Hi. 96732
871-8250

First Hawaiian Bank
20 W. Kaahumanu St.
Kahului, Hi. 96732
873-2275

SCHOOLS

Maui Community College
310 Kaahumanu Ave.
Kahului, Hi. 96732
984-3500

St. Anthony Catholic School
1618 E. Main St.
Wailuku, Hi. 96793
244-4190

Seabury Hall
480 Olinda Rd.
Makawao, Hi. 96768
572-7235

FOOD & LIQUOR WHOLESALERS

HFM Food Service
320 Hoohana St., Ste. 18
Kahului, Hi. 96732
871-5863

S. Hamasaki Wholesale Co., Ltd.
Wailuku, Hi. 96793
244-4996

Paradise Beverages
821 Eha St.
Wailuku, Hi. 96793
244-3144

SUPERMARKETS

Foodland
Kaahumanu Shopping Centerrr
Kahului, Hi. 96732
877-2808
In Lahaina
840 Wainee St.
Lahaina, Hi. 96761
661-0975
In Kihei
1881 S. Kihei Rd.
Kihei, Hi. 96753
879-9350

Ooka Supermarket
1870 Main St.
Wailuku, Hi. 96793
244-3931

Safeway
In Kahului
170 E. Kamehameha Ave.
Kahului, Hi. 96732
877-3377
In Lahaina
1221 Honoapiilani Hwy.
Lahaina, Hi. 96761
667-4392

MEDICAL

Maui Memorial Hospital
221 Mahalani St.
Wailuku, Hi. 96793
244-9056

Kula Sanitarium
204 Kula Hwy.
Kula, Hi. 96790
878-1221

Kaiser
80 Mahalani St.
Wailuku, Hi. 96793
243-6000

Clinical Labs
1831 Wili Pa Loop
Wailuku, Hi. 96793
244-5567

TOUR & TRAVEL AGENCIES

Pleasant Hawaiian Holidays
Desks at many resorts
667-2786

Roberts Hawaii Tours
871-6226

Tedeschi Vineyards
878-6058

Trans Hawaiian Services
711 Kaonawai Pl.
Kahului, Hi. 96732
877-7308

Trilogy Excursions
180 Lahanaluna Rd.
Lahaina 96761
661-4743

Maui Tropical Plantation
1670 Honoapiilani Hwy.
Wailuku, Hi. 96793
244-7643

DIVERSIFIED AGRICULTURE

Maui Land & Pineapple Co., Inc.
120 W. Kane
Kahului, Hi. 96732
877-3351

Pioneer Mill Co., Ltd.
380 Lahainaluna Rd.
Lahaina, Hi. 96761
661-3106

Hawaiian Commercial & Sugar Co.
Box 266
Puunene., Hi. 96784
877-0081

COMPUTER TECHNOLOGY

Maui High Performance Computer Center
550 Lipoa Pkwy. Ste. 100
Kihei, Hi. 96753
879-5077

UTILITIES

Maui Electric Co., Ltd.
210 W. Kamehameha Ave.
Kahului, Hi. 96732
871-8461

SECURITY GUARDS

Freeman Guards
900 Eha, Ste. 201
Wailuku, Hi. 96793
1-800-509-1588

Burns International Security Services
270 Hookahi, Ste. 312
Wailuku, Hi. 96793
244-7579

KAUAI

TOURIST INDUSTRY

HOTELS

Kauai Marriott
3610 Rice St.
Lihue, Hi. 96766
245-5050

Princeville Hotel
5520 Ka Haku Rd.
Princeville, Hi. 96722
826-9644

Sheraton Kauai Hotel
2440 Hoonani Rd.
Koloa, Hi. 96756
742-1661

Hyatt Regency
1571 Poipu Rd.
Koloa, Hi. 96756
742-1234
Embassy Resort
1613 Pee Rd.
Koloa, Hi. 96756
742-2823

Aston
4-484 Kuhio Hwy.
Kapaa, Hi. 96746
822-3441

Aston Kaha Lani
4460 Nehe Rd.
Kapaa, Hi. 96746
822-9331

Kiahuna Plantation
2253 Poipu Rd.
Koloa, Hi. 96756
742-2200

Outrigger Kauai Beach Hotel
4331 Kauai Beach Drive
Lihue, Hi. 96766
245-1955

Holiday Inn Sun Spree Resort
3-5920 Kuhio Hwy.
Kapaa, Hi. 96746
823-6000

TOUR & TRAVEL AGENTS

Roberts Hawaii Tours
3-4567 KuhioHwy
Lihue, Hi. 96766
245-5682

Waialeale Boat Tours, Inc.
Wailua Marina
822-4908

South Seas Tours & Helicopters
Lihue Airport
245-2222

Coconut Coast Activities
4-369A Kuhio Ave.
Kapaa, Hi. 96746
821-0015

Brennecke's Beach Center
2100 Hoone Rd.
Koloa, Hi. 96756
742-7505

STORES & DRUGSTORES

K Mart
4303 Nawiliwili St.
Lihue, Hi. 96766
245-7742

Wal Mart
33-300 Kuhio Hwy.
Lihue, Hi. 996766
246-1599

Liberty House
3-2600 Kaumualii Hwy.
Lihue, Hi. 96766
245-7751

Sears Roebuck & Co.
3-2600 Kaumualii Hwy.
Lihue, Hi. 96766
246-8301

Longs Drug Stores
3-2600 Kaumualii Hwy.
Lihue, Hi. 96766
245-7771

BOOKSTORES

Borders
4303 Nawiliwili Rd.
Lihue, Hi. 96766
246-0862

RESTAURANTS

Gaylord's
3-2087 Kaumualii Hwy.
Lihue, Hi. 96766
245-9593

Duke's Canoe Club
Kauai Marriott Hotel
3610 Rice St.
Lihue, Hi.

Chuck's Steak House
Princeville Center
Princeville, Hi. 96722
826-6211

Wranglers Steakhouse
9852 Kaumualii Hwy.
Waimea, Hi. 96796
338-1218

JJ's Broiler
3416 Rice St.
Lihue, Hi. 96766
246-4422

Kalapaki Beach Hut
3474 Rice St.
Lihue, Hi. 96766
246-6330

Roy's Poipu Bar & Grill
2360 Kiahuna Plantation Dr.
Koloa, Hi. 96756
742-5000

SUPERMARKETS

Big Save Inc.
444 Rice St.
Lihue, Hi. 96766
245-6571
six markets in various locations around the island

Foodland Super Market
Princeville, Hi .96722
826-9880
In Waipouli Town Center
822-7271

Safeway
4-831 Kuhio Hwy.
Lihue, Hi. 96766
822-2464

Star Markets
Kukui Grove Center
Lihue, Hi. 96766
245-7777

FOOD & LIQUOR WHOLESALERS

Koa Trading Co.
2975 Aukele St.
Lihue, Hi. 96766
245-6961

Better Brands
3071 Aukele St.
Lihue, Hi. 96766
245-4734
Paradise Beverages
3083 Aukele St. 96766
Lihue, Hi.
245-6938

Cereal & Fruit Products
3071 Aukele St. 96766
Lihue, Hi.
245-4734

Southern Wine & Spirits of Hawaii
1544 Haleukana Bay 2
Lihue, Hi. 96766
245-2999

BUILDING CONTRACTORS

Pacific Masonry
P. O. Box 1015
Koloa, Hi. 96756
742-9798

Werner Construction
P. O. Box 1134
Kalaheo, Hi. 96741
332-9919

Kauai Builders, Ltc.
3988 Halau St.
Lihue, Hi. 96766
245-2911

Curtis E. Law, Inc.
3271-1 Rice St.
Lihue, Hi. 96766
246-0676

Kauai Vinyl Siding Supply & Contracting Corp.
3-1856J Kaumualii Hwy.
Lihue, Hi. 96766
245-8454

MEDICAL

Wilcox Memorial Hospital
3420 Kuhio Hwy.
Lihue, Hi. 96766
245-1100

Samuel Mahelona Memorial Hospital
4800 Kawaihau Rd.
Kapaa, Hi. 96746
822-4961

West Kauai Medical Center
4643 Waimea Canyon Dr.
Waimea, Hi. 96796
338-9431

DIVERSIFIED AGRICULTURE

Kalihiwai Hydroponics Corp.
P. O. Box 947
Kilauea, Hi. 96754
828-1235

Gay & Robinson, Inc.
P. O. Box 156
Kaumakani, Hi. 96747
335-3133

Kauai Coffee Co.
P. O. Box 8
Eleele, Hi. 96705
335-5497

American Factors
2970 Kele
Lihue, Hi. 96766
245-7325

UTILITIES

Kauai Electric Co.
4463 Pahee St.
Lihue, Hi. 96766
246-4300

OAHU

TOURIST INDUSTRY

HOTELS

Ala Moana Hotel
410 Atkinson Dr.
Honolulu, Hi. 96814
955-4811

Waikiki Parkside Hotel
1850 Ala Moana
Honolulu, Hi. 96815

Hilton Hawaiian Village Hotel
2005 Kalia Road
Honolulu, Hi. 96815
949-4321

Hale Koa Hotel
2055 Kalia Rd.
Honolulu, Hi. 96815
955-0555

Holiday Inn Waikiki
1830 Ala Moana Blvd.
Honolulu, Hi. 96815
955-1111

Holiday Inn Airport
3401 N. Nimitz Hwy.
Honolulu, Hi. 96819
836-0661

Hawaii Prince
100 Holomoana
Honolulu, Hi. 96815

Best Western
3253 N. Nimitz Hwy.
Honolulu, Hi. 96819
836-3636

Hyatt Regency
2424 Kalakaua Ave.
Honolulu, Hi. 96815
923-1234

Ilikai Hotel
1777 Ala Moana Blvd.
Honolulu, Hi. 96815
949-3811

Kaimana Beach Hotel
2863 Kalakaua Ave.
Honolulu, Hi. 96815
923-1555

Queen Kapiolani Hotel
150 Kapahulu Ave.
Honolulu, Hi. 96815
922-1941

Sheraton
2155 Kalakaua Ave.
Honolulu, Hi. 996815
931-8292

Ihilani Resort & Spa
92-1001 Olani St.
Kapolei, Hi. 96707
679-0079

Castle Resorts
1150 S. King St.
Honolulu, Hi. 96814
591-2235

Aston Hotels
2155 Kalakaua Ave. #500
Honolulu, Hi. 96815
931-1400

Hawaiiana Hotel
444 Niu St.
Honolulu, Hi. 96815
923-3811

Marc Resorts
2155 Kalakaua 7th Floor
Honolulu, Hi. 96815
926-5900

Outrigger Hotels
2375 Kuhio Ave.
Honolulu, Hi. 96815
921-6600

Pacific Beach Hotel
2490 Kalakaua Ave.
Honolulu, Hi. 96815
922-1233

Pagoda Hotel
1525 Rycroft St.
Honolulu, Hi. 96814
941-6611

Park Shore Hotel
2586 Kalakaua Ave.
Honolulu, Hi. 96815
923-0411

Royal Hawaiian Hotel
440 Olohana
Honolulu, Hi. 96815
923-7311

Turtle Bay Hilton
57-091 Kamehameha Hwy.
Kahuku, Hi. 96731
293-8811

RESTAURANTS

Chief's Hut
Poolside at Outrigger Reef Hotel
Waikiki Beach
924-4992

Compadres
Ward Center
1200 Ala Moana Blvd.
Honolulu, Hi. 96814
591-8307

Ryan's Grill
Ward Center
1200 Ala Moana Blvd.
Honolulu, Hi. 96814
591-9132

Crouching Lion
51-666 Kamehameha Hwy.
Kaaawa, Hi. 96730
237-8511

Davy Jones Ribs
250 Lewers St.
Honolulu, Hi. 96815
923-7427

Godfather's Spinners Fun Bar & Grill
2463 Kuhio Ave.
Honolulu, Hi. 96815
923-5538

Jameson's
62-540 Kamehameha Hwy.
Haleiwa, Hi. 96712
637-4336

John Dominis
43 Ahui St.
Honolulu, Hi. 96813
523-0955

Matteo's
364 Seaside Ave.
Honolulu, Hi. 96815
922-5551

Nick's Fishmarket
2070 Kalakaua Ave.
Honolulu, Hi. 96815
955-6333

Sunset Terrace
Outrigger Hotel Waikiki Beach
971-3595

Trattoria
Edgewater Hotel
2168 Kalia Road
Honolulu, Hi. 96815
923-8415

Benihana of Tokyo
2005 Kalia Rd.
Honolulu, Hi. 96815
955-5955

Anna Miller's
98-115 Kaonohi St.
Aiea, Hi. 96701
487-2421

Buzz's Steak House
413 Kawailoa Rd.
Kailua, Hi. 96734
261-4661

Buzz's Steak & Lobster
225 Saratoga Road
Honolulu, Hi. 96815
923-6762

Chart House
1765 Ala Moana Blvd.
Honolulu, Hi. 96815
941-6669

Chart House
46-336 Haiku Rd.
Kaneohe, Hi. 96744
247-6671

Columbia Inn
645 Kapiolani Blvd.
Honolulu, Hi. 96813
596-0757

Columbia Inn
3221 Waialae Ave.
Honolulu, Hi. 96816
732-3663

Denny's Restaurant
2586 Kalakaua Ave.
Honolulu, Hi. 96815
926-7200

Denny's
205 Lewers St.
Honolulu, Hi. 96815
923-8188

Denny's
2345 Kuhio Ave.
Honolulu, Hi. 96815
922-9522

Denny's
Pearlridge Shopping Center
Aiea, Hi. 96701
488-6311

Dixie's
404 Ward Ave.
Honolulu, Hi. 96814
596-83359

Duke's
2335 Kalakaua #116
Honolulu, Hi. 96815
922-2268

Fisherman's Wharf
1009 Ala Moana
Honolulu, Hi. 96814
538-3808

Hee Hing
449 Kapahulu Ave.
Honolulu, Hi. 96815
734-8474

Kenny's Burger House
1620 N. School St.
Honolulu, Hi. 96817
841-0931

McDonald's Restaurants
711 Kapiolani Blvd. #1600
Honolulu, Hi. 96813
591-2080

Moose McGillycuddy's
310 Lewers St.
Honolulu, Hi. 96815
923-0751

Monterey Bay Canners
98-1005 Moanalua Rd.
Aiea, Hi. 96701
483-3555

Original Pancake House
1414 Dillingham Blvd.
Honolulu, Hi. 96817
847-1496

Ruth's Chris Steak House
1200 Ala Moana Blvd.
Honolulu, Hi. 96814
591-9132

TGI Friday
950 Ward Ave.
Honolulu, Hi. 96814
523-5841

Outback Steak House Hawaii
1778 Ala Moana Blvd.
Honolulu, Hi. 96815
951-6274

Tony Roma's
1972 Kalakaua
Honolulu, Hi. 96815
942-2121

Tony Roma's
4320 Waialae Ave.
Honolulu, Hi. 96816
735-9595

Tony Roma's
98-150 Kaonihi St.
Aiea, Hi. 96701
487-7427

Wailana Coffee Shop
1860 Ala Moana Blvd.
Honolulu, Hi. 96815
955-3736

STORES & DRUGSTORES

Costco
333A Keahole St.
Honolulu, Hi. 96825
396-5538

Costco
4380 Lawehana St.
Honolulu, Hi. 96818
422-6955

J. C. Penney
98-1025 Moanalua Rd.
Aiea, Hi. 96701

J. C. Penney
1450 Ala Moana Blvd.
Honolulu, Hi. 96814
946-8068

K Mart
500 N. Nimitz Hwy
Honolulu, Hi. 96817
528-2280
In Waipahu
94-825 Lumiaina St.
Waipahu, Hi. 96797
676-8886
At Salt Lake
4561 Salt Lake Blvd.
Honolulu, Hi. 96818
486-6118

Liberty House
Ala Moana Shopping Center
Honolulu, Hi. 96814
941-2345

Downtown
1032 Fort St. Mall
Honolulu, Hi. 96813
941-2345
Windward
Windward Mall
Kaneohe, Hi. 96744
941-2345
Kahala
4211 Waialae Ave.
Honolulu, Hi. 96816
941-2345
Pearlridge
Pearlridge Shopping Center
Aiea, Hi. 96701
9941-2345

There are about two dozen Long's Drug Stores scattered about the city. This address is their main administrative office:

Long's Drug Store
1088 Bishop St.
Honolulu, Hi. 96813
536-4551

Neiman Marcus
1450 Ala Moana #2101
Honolulu, Hi. 96814
951-8887

There are seven Ross stores in various locations.
Ross Stores
1000 Kamehameha Hwy
Pearl City, Hi. 96782
456-1005

Sam's Club
1000 Kamehameha Hwy. #100
Pearl City, Hi. 96782
456-7788

Sears Roebuck
450056 Kamehameha Hwy.
Kaneohe, Hi. 96744
247-8211

Sears Robuck
1450 Ala Moana Blvd.
Honolulu, Hi. 96814
947-0211

Sears Roebuck
Windward Mall
Kaneohe, Hi. 96744
247-8211

Sears Roebuck
98-180 Kamehameha Hwy
Aiea, Hi. 96701
487-4211

Sears Roebuck
98-600 Kamehameha Hwy
Pearl City, Hi. 96782
453-3500

Shirokiya
1450 Ala Moana Blvd.
Honolulu, Hi. 96814
973-9111

Shirokiya
1450 Ala Moana Blvd.
Honolulu, Hi. 96888881444
973-9111

Wal Mart
94-595 Kupuohi St.
Waipahu, Hi. 996789

Wal Mart
95-550 Lanikuhana Ave.
Mililani, Hi. 96789
623-6744

Andrade
Box 2480
Honolulu, Hi. 96804
971-4200

Banana Republic
1450 Ala Moana Blvd.
Honolulu, Hi. 96814
955-2602

The Gap
1450 Ala Moana
Honolulu, Hi. 96814
949-1933

Hilo Hattie's
700 N. Nimitz Hwy
Honolulu, Hi. 96817
524-3966

Kramer's
1450 Ala Moana
Honolulu, Hi. 96814
951-0567

Nordstrom
1450 Ala Moana
Honolulu, Hi. 96814
973-4620

FOOD & LIQUOR WHOLESALERS

Aloha Shoyu Co.
96-1205 Waihona St.
Honolulu, Hi. 96819
456-1929

Frito-Lay of Hawaii
99-1260 Iwaena St.
Honolulu, Hi. 96819
487-1515

H & W Foods
1535 Colburn
Honolulu, Hi. 96819
832-0350

Y. Hata & Co.
285 Sand Island Access Rd.
Honolulu, Hi. 96819
845-3347

Kahua Beef
3131 Koapaka St.
Honolulu, Hi. 96819
836-2731

Nishimoto Trading Co.
331 Libby St.
Honolulu, Hi. 96819
832-7555

Noh Foods of Hawaii
220B Puuhale Rd.
Honolulu, Hi. 96819
841-0655

Taiyo Inc.
5 Sand Island Access Rd. Bldg. T913
Honolulu, Hi. 96819
832-4951

Wei Chuan Food
5 Sand Island Access Rd. Ste. 101
Honolulu, Hi. 968819
845-5577

Y H Trading Co.
720G Moowaa
Honolulu, Hi. 96819
848-2822

Better Brands
94-501 Kau St.
Honolulu, Hi. 96819
676-6100

Cereal & Fruit Products
94-501 Kau St.
Honolulu, Hi. 96819
676-6166

Paradise Beverages
94-1450 Moaniani
Waipahu, Hi. 96797
678-4000

Anheuser-Bush
99-877 Iwaena St.
Aiea, Hi. 96701
487-0055

BANKS, CREDIT UNION, SECURITIES

American Savings Bank
915 Fort St. Mall
Honolulu, Hi. 96813
531-6262

Bank of Hawaii
111 S. King St.
Honolulu, Hi. 96813
643-3888

Bank of Honolulu
841 Bishop St.
Honolulu, Hi. 96813
543-3700

Central Pacific Bank
220 S. King St.
Honolulu, Hi. 96813
544-0500

City Bank
201 Merchant St.
Honolulu, Hi. 96813
535-2595

First Hawaiian Bank
999 Bishop St.
Honolulu, Hi. 96813
525-7000

Hawaii National Bank
45 N. King St.
Honolulu, Hi. 96813
Associates Financial Services
98-751 Kuahao Pl. #200
Pearl City, Hi. 96782
486-8681

Dean Witter
1001 Bishop Pacific #1600
Honolulu, Hi. 96813
525-6900

Finance Factors
1164 Bishop St.
Honolulu, Hi. 96813
548-4940

GTE Employees Credit Union
1138 N. King St.
Honolullu, Hi. 96817
832-8700

GE Capital Hawaii
745 Fort St. Mall 18th Floor
Honolulu, Hi. 96813
527-8200

Hawaii Central Credit Union
681 S. King St.
Honolulu, Hi. 96813
531-8911

Hawaii State Employees Federal Credit Union
560 Halekauwila St.
Honolulu, Hi. 96813
536-7717

Hickam Federal Credit Union
40 Hickam St.
Honolulu, Hi. 96818
423-1391

Honolulu City Employees Credit Union

832 S. Hotel St.
Honolulu, Hi. 96813
531-3711

Honolulu Federal Employees Federal Credit Union
300 Ala Moana Blvd.
Honolulu, Hi. 96813
523-7037

Hawaiian Airlines Federal Credit Union
P. O. Box 30065
Honolulu, Hi. 96820
835-3344

Oahu Educational Employees Federal Credit Union
1226 College Walk
Honolulu, Hi. 96817

Pearl Harbor Federal Credit Union
295 7th St.
Honolulu, Hi. 96818
423-1331

University of Hawaii Federal Credit Union
2010 East West Rd.
Honolulu, Hi. 96822
983-5500

International Savings & Loan Association
201 Merchant St.
Honolulu, Hi. 96813
535-2700

Island Community Lending
201 Merchant St. #2120
Honolulu, Hi. 96813
545-1000

Merrill Lynch
1001 Bishop St. Pauahi PH
Honolulu, Hi. 96813
525-7300

Prudential Securities
500 Ala Moana #2-400
Honolulu, Hi. 96813
547-5200

Smith Barney
1099 Alakea St. FL23
Honolulu, Hi. 96814
946-1400

BUILDING CONTRACTORS

Allstate Building Contractors Inc.
1015 Aoloa Pl. Ste. 254
Kailua, Hi.96734
262-8544

Allstate Industries, Inc.
1200 Sand Island Pkwy.
Honolulu, Hi. 96819
841-2165

Alpha Pacific Inc.
1052 Puuwai St.
Honolulu, Hi. 96819
841-7779

Walter Y. Arakaki Inc.
1029 Puuwai St.
Honolulu, Hi. 96819
841-3327

Armstrong Builders, Inc.
80 Sand Island Access Rd., Ste. 209
Honolulu, Hi. 96819
848-2484

Nate Barzilay Construction
5 Sand Island Access Road Bldg T922
Honolulu, Hi. 96819
8845-5638

Hicks Homes
46-217 Kahuhipa St.
Kaneohe, Hi. 96744

Kurico Inc.
P. O. Box 2109
Pearl City, Hi. 96782
486-7581

William Beard Ltd.
P. O. Box 2189
Honolulu, Hi. 96805
591-0761

E. E. Black, Ltd.
650 Kakoi St.
Honolulu, Hi. 96819
836-0454

Blueprint Builders, Inc.
1125 N. King St. Rm. 203
Honolulu, Hi. 96819
847-1411

Environmental Contracting Pacific
99-1205 Halawa Valley St., Ste. 304
Aiea, Hi. 96701
487-8444

Bodell Construction
56-701 Kamehameha Hwy.
Kahuku, Hi. 96731
293-0609

Chase Pacific Corp.
560 N. Nimitz Hwy., Ste. 216B
Honolulu, Hi. 96817
538-6810

J. W. Inc.
630 Laumaka St.
Honolulu, Hi. 96819
841-5888

Key Construction Ltd.
50 - L Sand Island Access Rd.
Honolulu, Hi. 96819
842-3174

Yamada's Plumbing & Contracting
1827 Republican St.
Honolulu, Hi. 96819
845-1702

Crosspoint Construction
850 Mililani
Mililani, Hi. 96789
528-2288

Dawn Pacific Inc.
2016 Democrat
Honolulu, Hi. 96819
841-4242

Dillingham Construction Pacific, Ltd.
614 Kapahulu Ave.
Honolulu, Hi. 96815
735-3211

Duarte & Sons Building - Plumbing, Inc.
1924 Republican St.
Honolulu, Hi. 96819
845-0070

Dura/Constructors
1210D N. Nimitz Hwy.
Honolulu, Hi. 96817
521-9499

Fletcher Pacific Construction
707 Richards Ste. 400
Honolulu, Hi. 96813
533-5000

Flobel Construction
4018 Salt Lake Blvd.
Honolulu, Hi. 96819
422-1249

Friendly Isle Contracting & Equipment Co.
5 Sand Island Access Rd. Bldg. 920
Honolulu, Hi. 96819
845-3873

Jas. W. Glover
725 Kapiolani Ave. #326
Honolulu, Hi. 96813
591-8977

Hawaiian Dredging & Construction
614 Kapahulu Ave.
Honolulu, Hi. 96815
735-3211

Heide & Cook
1714 Kanakanui St.
Honolulu, Hi. 96819
841-6161

Morrisen Knudsen Corp.
91-252 Kuhela St.
Kapolei, Hi. 96707
682-2085

Oahu Construction Co.
3375 Koapaka St. #H490
Honolulu, Hi. 96819
836-2981

Robert M. Kaya Builders
525 Kokea St. Bldg B-3
Honolulu, Hi. 96817
845-6477

U. S. Pacific Builders
1001 Bishop St. #1250
Honolulu, Hi. 96813
523-8554

Walker Moody Construction Co.
2927 Mokumoa St.
Honolulu, Hi. 96819
839-2781

COMPUTER TECHNOLOGY

A-1 United Laser
679 Auahi St.
Honolulu, Hi. 96813
538-05544

AIS Computer Centers
1130 N. Nimitz Hwy. Ste. 130A
Honolulu, Hi. 96817
526-2859

Active Computers Inc.
7192 Kalanianiole Hwy., Ste. C122
Honolulu, Hi. 96825
396-6209

Advance Data Corp.
1613 Houghtailing
Honolulu, Hi. 96819
842-6589

Art & Science
2615 S. King St.Ste. 202
Honolulu, Hi. 96814
942-1160

Honcad Corp.
1000 Bishop St. Ste. 702
Honolulu, Hi. 96813
537-9607

Spec Systems Corp.
1088 Bishop St. Ste. 310
Honolulu, Hi. 96813
531-2511

Budget PC of Hawaii
866 Iwilei Rd. Ste. 212
Honolulu, Hi. 96813
531-0396

Byteware Inc.
1007 Dillingham Blvd. Ste. 107
Honolulu, Hi. 96819
847-0360

Comp USA
500 Ala Moana Blvd. #210
Honolulu, Hi. 96813
537-1355

Century Computers
537A Pensacola
Honolulu, Hi. 96813
596-0444

Busch Consulting Inc.
2357 S. Beretania Ste. C208
Honolulu, Hi. 96815
941-3695

DSSI
429 Cooke St.
Honolulu, Hi. 96814
591-2622

Geminitech
1329 Kalani Ste. 307
Honolulu, Hi. 96819
843-1000

Networks Inc.
500 Ala Moana
Honolulu, Hi. 96813
521-4638

West Tech Software
1001 Bishop St. Ste. 898
Honolulu, Hi. 96813
536-3601

Compucom Systems Inc.
500 Ala Moana, Ste. 400
Honolulu, Hi. 96813
533-1952

Compuskills
1221 Kapiolani . Ste. 230
Honolulu, Hi. 96813
596-0082

Computer City Supercenter
1108 Auahi St.
Honolulu, Hi. 96813
591-6300

Technology Integration Group
680 Ala Moana Blvd.
Honolulu, Hi. 96813
524-6652

Personal Touch Computers
311 Keawe St.
Honolulu, Hi. 96813
524-7253

Global Computing
98-1268 Kaahumanu St. Ste. 200
Pearl City, Hi. 96782
487-3475

Computer Resources Hawaii, Inc.
720 Iwilei Rd., Rm 210 Box 14
Honolulu, Hi. 96813
545-5770

Century Computers
537A Pensacola
Honolulu, Hi. 96813
596-00444

Wang Government Services, Inc.
354A Uluniu St., Ste. 203
Kailua, Hi. 96734
266-2000

Commercial Data Systems Inc.
50 S. Beretania, Ste. C208
Honolulu, Hi. 96813
527-2000

Data Care Technologies
1100 Alakea 26th Floor
Honolulu, Hi. 96813
524-3111

Fujitsu Systems
560 N. Nimitz Hwy. Ste. 214
Honolulu, Hi. 96817
524-7786

Computer House Inc.
111 Sand Island Access Rd. Rm 18
Honolulu, Hi. 96819
841-4848

Unisys Corp.
711 Kapiolani Blvd. Ste. 425
Honolulu, Hi. 96813
591-7000

DIVERSIFIED AGRICULTURE

Alexander & Baldwin
822 Bishop St.
Honolulu, Hi. 96813
525-6611

Amfac/JMB Hawaii
700 Bishop St. #2002
Honolulu, Hi. 96813
543-8900

Castle & Cooke
650 Iwilei Rd.
Honolulu, Hi. 96817
548-4811

Dole Food Company
1116 Whitmore Ave.
Wahiawa, Hi. 96786
621-3200

Del Monte
94-1000 Kunia Rd.
Kunia, Hi. 96759
621-1208

MEDICAL

Queen's Hospital
1301 Punchbowl St.
Honolulu, Hi. 96813
538-9011

Queen's Health System
1099 Alakea St. #1100
Honolulu, Hi. 96813
532-6100

St. Francis Hospital
2230 Liliha
Honolulu, Hi. 96817
547-6011

St. Francis Medical Center West
91-2141 Fort Weaver Rd.
Ewa Beach, Hi. 96706
678-7000

Kuakini Hospital
347 N. Kuakini St.
Honolulu, Hi. 96817
536-2236

Kapiolani Hospital
1319 Punahou
Honolulu, Hi. 96826
983-6000

Kapiolani at Pali Momi
98-1079 Moanalua Rd.
Aiea, Hi. 96701
486-6000

Kapiolani Health System
55 Merchant St. #2700
Honolulu, Hi. 96813
535-7401

Straub Clinic & Hospital
888 S. King St.
Honolulu, Hi. 96813

Kaiser Permanente
3288 Moanalua Rd.
Honolulu, Hi. 96819
834-9094

Kaiser Permanente
1010 Pensacola St.
Honolulu, Hi. 96814
545-2950

Kaiser Koolau Clinic
45-602 Kamehameha Hwy.
Kaneohe, Hi. 96744
235-7100

Kaiser Punawai Clinic
94-235 Leoku St.
Waipahu, Hi. 96797
677-5888

Castle Hospital
640 Ulukahiki St.
Kailua, Hi. 996734
263-5500

Wahiawa General Hospital
128 Lehua
Wahiawa, Hi. 96786
621-8411

Waianae Health Center
86-260 Farrington Hwy.
Waianae, Hi. 96792
696-7081

Rehabilitation Hospital of the Pacific
226 N. Kuakini St.
Honolulu, Hi. 96817
531-3511

Shriners Hospital for Crippled Children
1310 Punahou
Honolulu, Hi. 96826
941-4466
Maunalani Nursing Home
5113 Maunalani Circle
Honolulu, Hi. 96816
732-0771

Pohai Nani
45-090 Namoku St.
Kaneohe, Hi. 96744
247-6211

Beverly Manor
1930 Kamehameha IV Rd.
Honolulu, Hi. 96819
847-4834

Central Medical Clinic
321 N. Kuakini St. #201
Honolulu, Hi. 96817
523-8611

Hale Nani Rehabilitation & Nursing Center
1677 Pensacola St.
Honolulu, Hi. 96822
537-3371

Hawaiian Eye Center
606 Kilani Ave.
Wahiawa, Hi. 96786

Honolulu Medical Group
550 S. Beretania St.
Honolulu, Hi. 96813
537-2211

Kahi Mohala Hospital
91-2301 Fort Weaver Rd.
Ewa Beach, Hi. 96706
671-8511

Kalihi-Palama Mental Health Center
915 N. King St.
Honolulu, Hi. 96817
848-1438

Leahi Hospital
3675 Kilauea Ave.
Honolulu, Hi. 96816
733-8000

Tripler Army Medical Center
1 Jarrett White Rd.
Honolulu, Hi. 96859
433-6661

UTILITIES

The Gas Co.
515 Kamakee
Honolulu, Hi. 96814
535-5900

Gaspro
2305 Kamehameha Hwy.
Honolulu, Hi. 96819

Hawaiian Electric Co.
900 Richards St.
Honolulu, Hi. 968133
543-7771

Honolulu Disposal Service
P. O. Box 30968
Honolulu, Hi. 96820
845-7581

SECURITY

Freeman Guards
1130 N. Nimitz Hwy. #226
Honolulu, Hi. 96817
532-2944

Loomis Fargo
1540 Kalani St.
Honolulu, Hi. 96817
841-7511

Alert Alarm
1270 Queen Emma St.
Honolulu, Hi. 96813

Burns International Security Services
401 Waiakamilo Rd. #202
Honolulu, Hi. 96817
842-4800

Wackenhut Corporation
3375 Koapaka #D-105
Honolulu, Hi. 96819
839-1185

TOUR & TRAVEL AGENTS

Paradise Cove Luau
1580 Makaloa Ste. 1230
Honolulu, Hi. 96815
945-3571

Sand & Sea Activities Inc.
6806 Niumalu Loop
Honolulu, Hi. 96813
395-7263

Sea Life Park Hawaii
41-202 Kalanianaole Hwy.
Waimanalo, Hi. 96795
259-7993

Skydive Hawaii
68-760 Farrington Hwy.
Aiea, Hi. 96701

Waikiki Acquarium
2777 Kalakaua Ave.
Honolulu, Hi. 96815
923-9741

Affordable Tours
2440 Kuhio Ave. Ste. 1
Honolulu, Hi. 96815
922-5522

Char Tour & Travel Service
160 N. Hotel St.
Honolulu, Hi. 96814
538-7073

American Express Travel
1221 Kapiolani Blvd. #400
Honolulu, Hi. 96814
596-3700

Atlantis Submarines
1600 Kapiolani #1630
Honolulu, Hi. 96814
973-9800

Cheap Tickets
1440 Kapiolani #800
Honolulu, Hi. 96814

JTB Hawaii
2155 Kalakaua 9th Floor
Honolulu, Hi. 96815
922-0200
Pleasant Hawaiian Holidays
2222 Kalakaua Ave. 16th Floor
Honolulu, Hi. 96815
926-1833

Polynesian Adventure Tours
1049 Kikowaena Pl.
Honolulu, Hi. 96819
833-9600

Polynesian Cultural Center
55-370 Kamehameha Hwy.
Laie, Hi. 96762
293-3000

Regal Travel
720 Iwilei #101
Honolulu, Hi. 96817
566-7000

Roberts Hawaii Tours
680 Iwilei Rd. #700
Honolulu, Hi. 96817
523-7750

Trans Hawaiian Services
720 Iwilei Rd. #101
Honolulu, Hi. 96817
566-7000

SUPERMARKETS

Big Way Super Markets
94-340 Waipahu Depot
Waipahu, Hi. 96797
677-3171

Food Pantry Ltd.
3536 Harding Ave.
Honolulu, Hi. 96816
732-5515

Foodland
55-510 Kamehameha Hwy.
Laie, Hi. 96762
293-4443

Foodland Super Market
Ewa Beach Shopping Center
Ewa Beach, Hi. 96706
689-8383

Foodland Super Market
414 N. School St.
Honolulu, Hi. 96817
533-1398

Foodland Super Market
850 Kamehameha Hwy.
Pearl City, Hi. 96782
455-3213

Foodland Super Market
Windward City Shopping Center
Kaneohe, Hi. 96744
247-3357

Foodland Super Market
1450 Ala Moana Blvd.
Honolulu, Hi. 96814
949-5044

Foodland Super Market
1460 S. Beretania St.
Honolulu, Hi. 96814
946-4654

Foodland
1505 Dillingham
Honolulu, Hi. 9688817
845-2134

Foodland
2295 N. King St.
Honolulu, Hi. 96819
845-1249

Foodland
Aina Haina Shopping Center
Honolulu, Hi. 96821
373-2222

Foodland
Koko Marina Shopping Center
Honolulu, Hi. 96825
395-3131

Foodland
823 California Ave.
Wahiawa, Hi. 96786
621-7411

Foodland
59-720 Kamehameha Hwy.
Haleiwa, Hi. 96712
621-7411

Foodland
95-221 Kipapa Dr.
Mililani, Hi. 96789
623-3974

Foodland
94-1040 Waipio Uka St.
Waipahu, Hi. 96797
671-5322

Foodland
2939 Harding
Honolulu, Hi. 96816
734-6303

Star Market
2470 S. King St.
Honolulu, Hi. 96825

Star Market
1620 N. School St.
Honolulu, Hi. 96817
832-8400

Star Market
4211 Waialae Ave.
Honolulu, Hi. 96816
733-1366

Star Market
95-1249 Mehula Pkwy.
Mililani, Hi. 96789
625-7171

Safeway Supermarket
680 Iwilei Rd. #590
Honolulu, Hi. 96817
524-4554

Safeway
848 Ala Lilikoi St.
Honolulu, Hi. 96818
839-99681

Safeway
46-065 Kamehameha Hwy.
Kaneohe, Hi. 96744
235-3337

Safeway
25 Kaneohe Bay Dr.
Kailua, Hi. 96734
254-2597

Safeway
1060 Keolu Dr.
Kailua, Hi. 96734
261-1909

Safeway
200 Hamakua Dr.
Kailua, Hi. 96734
261-1909

Safeway
377 Keahole St.
Honolulu, Hi. 96825
396-6337

Safeway
98-1277 Kaahumanu St.
Aiea, Hi. 96701
487-1088

Safeway
1360 Pali Hwy.
Honolulu, Hi. 96813
538-3953

Safeway
1121 S. Beretania St.
Honolulu, Hi. 96814
591-8315

Safeway
94-780 Meheula Pky B
Honolulu, Hi. 96815
623-8111

Safeway
91-590 Farrington Hwy.
Kapolei, Hi. 96707
674-0070

Safeway
94-050 Farrington Hwy.
Waipahu, Hi. 96797
677-1555

Tamashiro Market
802 N. King St.
Honolullu, Hi. 96826
841-8047

Times Supermarket
94-766 Farrington Hwy.
Waipahu, Hi. 96797
671-0502

Times Supermarket
94-615 Kupuohi
Waipahu, Hi. 96797
678-6565

Times Supermarket
1173 21st Ave.
Honolulu, Hi. 96816
732-6677

Times Supermarket
3221 Waialae Ave.
Honolulu, Hi. 96816

Times Supermarket
2153 N. King St.
Honolulu, Hi. 96819
847-0811

Times Supermarket
1772 S. King St.
Honolulu, Hi. 96826
955-3388

Times Supermarket
99-115 Aiea Heights Dr.
Aiea, Hi. 96701

Times Supermarket
1290 Beretania St.
Honolulu, Hi. 96814
524-5711

Times Supermarket
1425 Liliha St.
Honolulu, Hi. 96817
536-4436

Times Supermarket
5740 Kalanianaole Hwy.
Honolulu, Hi. 96821
373-9883

Times Supermarket
98-1264 Kaahumanu St.
Pearl City, Hi. 96782
487-3687

Times Supermarket
47-388 Hui Iwa
Kaneohe, Hi. 96744
239-8827

Times Supermarket
45-934 Kamehameha Hwy.
Kaneohe, Hi. 96744

Times Supermarket
590 Kailua Rd.
Kailua, Hi. 96734
262-2366

SCHOOLS

University of Hawaii at Manoa
2530 Dole St.
Honolulu, Hi. 96822
956-8111

University of Hawaii
West Oahu
96-043 Ala Ike
Pearl City, Hi. 96782
453-6565

Windward Community College
45-720 Keaahala Rd.
Kaneohe, Hi. 96744
235-0077

Leeward Community College
96-045 Ala Ike
Pearl City, Hi. 96782
455-0011

Honolulu Community College
874 Dillingham
Honolulu, Hi. 96817
845-9211

Hawaii Pacific University
1166 Fort St. Mall
Honolulu, Hi. 96813
544-0200

Chaminade University
3140 Waialae Ave.
Honolulu, Hi. 96816
735-4711

Brigham Young University Hawaii
55-220 Kulanui St.
Laie, Hi. 96762
293-3211

Punahou School
1601 Punahou St.
Honolulu, Hi. 96822
944-5711

Iolani School
563 Kamoku St.
Honolulu, Hi. 96826
949-5355

Kamehameha Secondary School
210 Konia Circle
Honolulu, Hi. 96817
842-8211

St. Louis School
3142 Waialae Ave.
Honolulu, Hi. 96816
739-7777

St. Andrews Priory School
224 Queen Emma Square
Honolulu, Hi. 96813
536-6102

Sacred Hearts Academy
3253 Waialae Ave.
Honolulu, Hi. 96816
734-5058

About The Author

Written by a retired attorney who was born and grew up in Hawaii, whose ancestors settled in the islands in 1839.